Inmate 458627
A Man's story of Mental Health, Love, Hurt & Healing

Dr. Stephens,

Words can't express how much our friendship means!

I appreciate your loving spirit.

Rashad "Bowtie" Mills

Inmate 458627
A Man's story of Mental Health, Love, Hurt & Healing

Rashad Mills

Edited by Edward Robertson

2019

First Printing: 2019

ISBN 978-0-359-62408-9

Baltimore, Maryland

rashadmills.com

Ordering Information:

Special discounts are available on quantity purchases by corporations, associations, educators, and others. For details, contact the publisher at the above listed address.

U.S. trade bookstores and wholesalers:

Please contact Rashad Mills

Email rashadspeaks@rashadmills.com

Dedication

To my twins. You provided me with enough motivation to continue to make it through this journey.

God loves you. I love you. You're beautiful. You're smart and can have anything in the world if you work hard for it.

Contents

Preface

I have the greatest love for those who are suffering from mental illnesses of all kinds. As a therapist and someone who has suffered - I know that healing is possible. You are not alone in this journey. I honestly believe that we are as sick as the secrets that we hide. Healing comes from admitting that issues exist.

The Matters of The Heart

"Above all else, guard your heart, for everything you do flows from it" **Proverbs 4:23 (NIV)**

July 18, 2015, was a big day in my life because it marked the last time that I had a drink. I remember attending a concert in downtown Baltimore with a cousin of mine, and of course, I was drunk. My huge moment of embarrassment came when I bumped into one of my former professors from Morgan State University. Seeing that I was under the influence, as if, the slurring of my words wasn't enough—he sheepishly introduced me to his wife. Wonderful as she was back in school, she instantly remembered me. Her reflection of me was as the guy who my professor bragged to her that I was on my way to ESPN—as the next broadcasting sensation. He asked me why I haven't gotten back in the field of broadcast journalism (lost a sportscaster job in Oregon due to an alcohol-related accident) and I didn't have the courage to say that my life was a mess and I was spiraling out of control. I drive home drunk, and unfortunately, it was the norm for me after one of my drinking episodes. It was something about the moment when I entered the house that was different. I remember asking God to take the spirit of alcohol from me because I had wrecked parts of my life as a result of it. Apparently, he was listening.

Prior to that day, I had battled alcoholism, depression, self-esteem issues and even spent time in a psychiatric unit for two days after a failed relationship. I was at my wit's end trying to find different options that could help me get out of this funk and live a better life. The spirit in the bottle had a hold of me and refused to let go. It was the only coping skill, although unhealthy—that I could rely on to feel good momentarily. Quite frankly, I put in a lot of effort to make the relationship work despite the negative outcomes of it.

I had wrestled, on several occasions, with the idea of putting down the bottle—only to start again when the first problem arose that I was mentally unequipped to handle. It was a personal struggle that only a few people knew about. On several occasions, at the urging of others, I went to alcoholics anonymous, but I really wasn't ready to stop. One of the biggest hurdles that I have to overcome with the thought of actually being an alcoholic. It was an impossible term for me live with because I was simply a guy that liked to drink uncontrollably with his friends on the weekend. "*Alcoholic*" had such a negative meaning attached to it and I wasn't in that category. My sense of arrogance, pride, and selfishness would not take AA meetings seriously. My mind was programmed to believe that those other people are "drunks," but I'm different. Many of the people who thought they knew me viewed as a "party boy" but in actuality, it was a show and a big act to throw people off from the mental hurt that I was experiencing, On several occasions—I would get home after nights out with my friends and feel so disgusted inside that I would wash sleeping medicine down with liquor. I can honestly say now that the sleep aids served more as a method to quiet my mind, as opposed to helping with the potential hangover. Due to the years of drinking, my tolerance levels grew higher—as did the raw feelings of worthlessness. Alcohol could no longer substitute for the real healing that I needed so desperately.

In my opinion, the church is the best place to turn in getting the desired help for any problem. As a kid, my mother laid a foundation and the church was the center of it. She always made sure that my brother and I were up pretty early and ready for worship. Since I was the more vocal of her sons, she decided to have me more involved with the junior ushers, a busy job involving escorting people to their seats. I was not opposed to being an usher until I had to usher the later services which interfered with the Sunday NFL games. At that time, I loved the Philadelphia Eagles more than God.

Throughout the roller coaster of my life, I always knew God would bring back me to church. The church is often referred to as "the hospital" and I was sick! Sick of not feeling fulfilled in multiple areas of my life. Since I hadn't been to church in a while, I decided to attend a church with a Pastor I was already familiar with. This Pastor had a unique preaching style that I gravitated towards. I recall following the Pastor going to the church when it was located in a much smaller venue about 8-10 year prior. Since that time the church has relocated to a bigger congregational space, on the outskirts of Baltimore County. I remember leaving clubs, partying, drinking, going home, sleeping and showering—then running back out to church. Even in the midst of my crazier days—I knew I couldn't continually run from God. I felt like I was walking the line of trying to do the right thing and still have my kind of fun.

If the church is the hospital, then Jesus must be the doctor. The church becomes a place of comfort for me, as my soul attempted to heal from the interpersonal problems that I was dealing with. Each message that was preached, felt like it was made, specifically for me. I felt a change occurring in my life as a result of developing a deeper connection with God.

With each Sunday that I attended service—I noticed the spirit of God was moving me closer to Him. Also, I noticed my flesh was being drawn to a gorgeous woman in the church. It was interesting because I would find myself peeking over at her during the service and asking God to forgive me for my lack of concentration. One of the things that I was immediately drawn to was her beautiful dark chocolate complexion. In addition to this—she was always immaculately dressed from head to toe. Her athletic build and height (probably 6 feet tall) gave me the impression that she was a former basketball player. She had the straightest teeth I had ever seen and of the most interesting eye colors ever. On many a day, she could be seen wearing bright orange wire framed designer glasses, a short-layered do hair, manicured nails, which appeared to be done every week. What really got my attention was the way that she praised God. At that point—I saw her really connecting with God and she seemed to have a love for her position in the church as a minister and her calling to serve God's people.

She was an integral part of assisting newer people getting educated about the church. Fortunately for me I experienced this first hand. Week after week had passed and I found myself lying in the church. When the Pastor asked if people were saved—I would look down so no one would have the opportunity to look at me and ask. If they did look at me and ask—I would say with a high level of confidence that, Yes, I'm saved. Pastor was so compelling and would use the line, *"If you take one step—Almighty God will take the rest."* Moved in the spirit, I got up and took that step towards my salvation. And of course, she was the one who took my hand and led me to the back. I was dressed in black slacks, black dress pants, and a fashionable bowtie. I was entirely focused on God—but she mentioned how nice my bowtie was—I almost passed out right there in church! As she led me to prayer and provided me with information about the church—I quickly noticed two things: she had a walk that exuded sheer confidence and a mellifluous fragrance that was most pleasing to my senses.

I would see her Sunday after Sunday but I didn't have the courage to say anything. To be honest, my confidence was at an all-time low after my last relationship. Under the smile and bowties was an individual who was afraid to enter a relationship again. When I would look at her, I would begin to have an internal battle that said, *"Rashad you are not good enough."* As a result of this faulty thinking—I wouldn't think about saying anything to her. I was questioning my readiness for friendship, companionship or a relationship. I would ask myself is this what I need at the moment? Attractive women have been the biggest distraction of my life. I had always operated from a scarce mentality. The mentality that says a successful, attractive woman is the last person on earth that would desire me.

To be honest, I wasn't sure that I was fully healed from my previous relationship. It was the equivalent of trying to take a band-aid off of a cut and the wound is still raw, even despite all of the personal development that I had completed. However—the thought of connecting with God first and to then having someone to take the journey with was an amazing thought. I needed so much of God that I was a regular at Sunday morning services (7:30am and 9:30am) middle aisle, second row, first seat to the far left and for Tuesday Bible study. I had to stay focused because I had a major professional hurdle to face.

Towards the end of 2015, I was studying for a national counseling exam that I needed to pass in order to get closer to being a licensed clinical professional counselor. I vividly remember one weekend I set outside for the purpose of studying for this test. On a particular Friday evening, I was on the way home and stopped to get some food. I figured if I was going to be in the house that I might as well have a full stomach. As I exited my favorite restaurant, I got in my car and I noticed that it won't start. Oh Boy! My mind immediately begins to think about doom and gloom. Why Me? Why Now? God, why would you allow this to happen! After sitting in the car with the highest-level anxiety imaginable—I quickly shifted to realize that I had to do something fast but I knew my car couldn't stay where it was and I know the importance of having a working vehicle. AAA came to my rescue with quick towing. The following day, I called several auto parts stores and frantically searched for the car part with the hopes that my uncle will be able to fix it. My cousin drove me around Baltimore City all day long and I was unsuccessful until the final call that I decided to make.

FINALLY!!! The part was available and my cousin got me to the store in record-breaking time. She drives like a NASCAR driver and gives meaning to the phrase, *"Ride or Die."* Now half of the equation was taken care of but the next question was, "Would my uncle be able to care of it?" At this point, it was already dark and my uncle is the greatest mechanic known to man, but without access to a shop and adequate lighting- the job is extra difficult. As I paced back and forth in my grandmother's house–God said let there be light, so in walks my uncle wearing some contraption on his head that resembled a miner in the cave, light included. Before I could even thank him for his efforts, he was already out the door to start on my car. I was incredibly relieved!! At this time—I received a phone call from an unidentified number and I started not to answer it, but my better judgment told me to do so. My life changed when I answered the phone. *"Good Evening, may I speak with Rashad, please?'"* And I replied, *"this is him, and who am I speaking with?"* She told me her name and that she was a minister from the church. She asked if I was still interested in getting baptized. And of course—I replied, *"Yes!"* Due to the increased stress level that I was under - her voice (I detected some type of southern accent) felt so good to my ears at the moment. I can't quite remember the exact words that were said next but I do remember her making a joke and I was laughing. She told me what time to be at the church and our call ended. It was the perfect culmination to a day filled with stress and frustration. Now my concern went back to the status of my car. Within a matter of minutes—my uncle walked back in the house and handed me my keys and said, *"You are all done."* My level of excitement had gone to the next level because things, in a short period were slowly falling into place. As I drove home-my thoughts shifted to what suit I would wear for my baptismal the next day.

As I sat in the church parking lot the next day, my stomach gave me all kind of discomfort. Prior to major events occurring in my life, I always have an interesting feeling in my stomach. It wasn't the sensation of fear or medical attention, or the need to use the restroom. I just know something meaningful was about to take place. I walked in the fellowship hall—early of course—because I dislike tardiness so much. For roughly 45 minutes or so—It was killing time but looking at my phone, and then she walked in from a back door, apparently from her office. I didn't see her walk in but I noticed her when I looked up and she was wearing a grey business suit with a pair of burgundy heels. Whew! Such a beauty and with class. She was working on a list—I'm assuming she was verifying and checking the names of the individuals who were going to be baptized. She looked up and said, *"Good Morning Sir, are you nervous?"* Inside, I was even more nervous now because she was talking to me. It was almost the equivalent of schoolboy talking to his crush in the cafeteria. I replied a little and I said, *"Were you the young lady who called me last night?* And she smiled and replied, *"Yes I am."* At this point- other members were walking in and I was in awe of the way she interacted with everyone. She appeared to have a genuine spirit and an even bigger heart. Her energy was friendly and warm with everyone. After being baptized by the Pastor— I remember walking down from the pulpit feeling so good about what just occurred, by at same at the same time, trying to get to know this young lady on a deeper level. I saw one of my longtime friends who was working at the church at the time and I said to her, guess who I have a crush on? Before I could finish my statement, she said, *"I know exactly who you are talking about."* My friend told me that I will introduce you to her. I screamed NO!!!

She was described as a woman of God and an excellent mother. She began asking about why I'm in the process of getting myself together. With this one question the coming weeks would yield many opportunities to see her and speak—but I didn't have the game to approach her. I feel like it was playing Double-Dutch—ready to jump in and then jump back out. Finally—it was time to see if I still had it. It was around Valentine's Day when I was ready to approach her. My friend had already done all of the work that she could possibly do. I was with my twins in Sunday school when I saw that she started speaking with them. Then she and I begin to briefly converse and she mentioned that she "heard" that I wanted to talk to her. My heart was beating at a ridiculously rapid rate. *Was my church crush about to reject me?* And all of a sudden—I was saved by the start of Sunday school.

I just smiled and gave thanks to God for the brief reprieve. The overthinker in me began to wonder why she wasn't married or involved in a relationship. She appeared to have the surefire characteristics of a woman that any guy would like to be with. My inquisitive nature led me to reach out to one of the guys in the church that I knew. He advised me that other guys have made an effort to date her, but they were all unsuccessful. When I asked about why—he stated after the initial conversation—she would often forget that the conversations ever occurred. That struck me as really odd but not enough to deter me.

He mentioned an interaction in which he spoke to her and she viewed him as being flirtatious and she violently cursed him out. He stated that he has never spoken with her since. The last thing he told me was alarming; but I treated it casually and didn't place the proper amount of emphasis on it. He shared that she has been known to be mentally unstable—a definite red flag—based on some of her behaviors. Before I could offer a rebuttal, he laughed and said, *"Oh you'll be fine because you will know how to handle her as a therapist."* I would find out later exactly what he meant.

Eventually—I felt her eyes looking at me more often during the future services. There was no way to found out about her but to approach her again. I remember one Sunday that she arrived right after me which was strange because I arrived 30 minutes before the service starts. She went to the altar and knelt down and begin to pray with such passion. It was such a sight to see such a beautiful praying woman. Due to my natural intuition and being counseling in training—I instantly knew something wasn't right. For instance, a week later I realized that I was 100% correct. I went to approach her after the church service in an effort to get her phone number. She was visibly distressed, as evidenced by her facial expression. During a very short conversation, she stated that she couldn't think at the moment because her brother had recently passed. My heart literally dropped to the floor. All the lines that I prepared to get her number evaporated into thin air. As I drove home—I was saddened for her because I couldn't fathom what she was experiencing. Since I didn't officially know her, I wasn't sure what I could do. I did a little detective work and found out which flowers were appropriate for that kind of moment; I couldn't go wrong with the right flowers and a card. I picked out the best of the choice of flowers and wrote *Blessed are those who mourn, for they shall be comforted.* (**Matthew 5:4.** *NIV)*. I didn't how to sign it, so it was written—*Sincerely, Rashad, your brother in Christ.* It was delivered to the church and she received it and was totally surprised and apparently grateful. So grateful in fact, that she wanted to get my number and thank me. When I heard this—my heart jumped for joy. I wanted to show appropriate measure and remain sincere with my condolences.

I patiently waited to get the call and nothing ever happened. Around this time—I was asked to be in a church play and I was spending more time in church. Life was slowly but surely turning around in my favor. On one Monday night—I vividly remember preparing to rehearse my lines when my phone rang. It was a number that I was unfamiliar with. I said, *Hello, Hello* and the person hangs up. I called right back and didn't receive an answer. Strangely enough—I received a text message from the same number stating who she was and she was thankful for the flowers. I thought it was odd that a text was sent but a refusal was given to speaking on the phone.

The days and weeks that followed, we played phone tag until we landed on the same accord enough to have a conversation. Most of the conversations were 20 minutes and inconsistent at best. I prayed to God to show me if I was wasting my time. I fasted and prayed and on the last day of my fast—she called. She mentioned that she was sick for the last few days, due to a new vitamin that she was taking. Of course—I felt bad that she was sick, but I was elated because I thought this was surely a sign from God that she was the one. Even though we weren't in a relationship—I was really feeling her. On the way to the church for another play rehearsal—I went to the store next to the church and bought up any and all medications possible. I placed them in a nice basket and give it to my friend to forward to her. Again, she seemed so appreciative at my thoughtfulness.

The short conversations turned into long (sometimes four hours) in depth, meaningful talks, in which no one wanted to get off of the phone. It was similar to a teenage love story. She was everything that I could have ever wanted. Prior to meeting her, one of my friends encouraged me to write down the list of qualities that I wanted in a woman. I had a list of the things and not in any specific order—loves God, accepts my past as less than a perfect person, doesn't drink, accept my kids, good spirited, etc. This was too good to be true. Doing one phone conversation she told me that she hadn't seriously dated since her divorce in 2011 and she just wanted to "find a man who loved God more than her." In addition to this—she stated (why I'm not sure) that she likes to flirt with other men and she won't affirm a man. It was slightly confusing as to why she would say things like that. We begin to go out on more dates and spend more time together. One particular date stood out more than others. We had a meal at a restaurant that is adjacent to a beautiful lake. The lake serves as the perfect place for an after dinner romantic walk. And that's exactly what we did. It was perfect because I disclosed to her my past struggles with alcoholism and my past relationship struggles. There was a high level of comfortability and openness sharing this information with her. I wanted to be upfront, honest and not have any secrets, even though we weren't officially a couple. As we exited the lake—she told me to drive her truck back to her house. I quickly obliged without a second thought. As soon as I got in—I noticed that the gas was low and I headed to the nearest gas station before getting on the highway.

After paying for gas, gum and two bottled waters; I filled up the tank. As soon as I got back in the truck—she showed me her phone and said—he just texted me. I responded, who are you talking about? She said it's The Pastor of the church. She leaned and over showed me the text. "*I just wanted to check on you.*" The name was saved in her phone with his initials. At this time—It was getting closer to 10:30pm. My natural gut instinct told me that something wasn't right. My experience with dating and woman quickly reminded me that, "*I just wanted to check on you*" had a different meaning behind it. All that being said, I didn't want to make assumptions. It wasn't a text for a last-minute prayer call. She was adamant that he makes an effort to contact her and she doesn't engage for the fear of her position to be affected. I gave her the benefit of the doubt to avoid my past trust and insecurity issues surfacing. We moved past this without further mention but my senses were always on guard, as it would later resurface.

Other than God and my kids, there was no one else that I spent as much time with. But it was great!!! We were keeping each other accountable for reading the Bible. I was trying to read the entire Bible in one year. Normally, I would get ahead of her in the readings. She would get sidetracked with the book of Job because she loved how Job was restored after losing everything. God was such a part of our relationship and I loved it. On many nights—she would pray for me as no woman has ever done. I felt like I loved her but wasn't going to be the first one to say it.

Less than 3 months into the relationship, I remember her telling me that she had something to tell me. She said three of the most powerful words on the face of the planet—*I love you*, however, the way she did it came off as a bit odd to me. We were laying on the couch enjoying each other company and she mumbled some words. I asked her, what did you say? She said "*I love you,*" but it was meant for my daughter. I was confused because my daughter wasn't present at the moment. She described it as something that she is used to saying to her daughter. That was the first of many instances that I noticed she struggled with expressing her emotions, which at that time wasn't alarming. Fireworks were going off in my mind and my heart. It was so early in the relationship and we hadn't had the opportunity to discover each other but it felt like love to me. It was the perfect match because she gives me the chance to led as a man and I was validated. That was so refreshing for me because in previous relationships—I operated from a boy's mentality and not as a man.

For the first time in my life, I was so excited to take on the responsibility of trying to fix things around the house and take the lead. One of the coolest moments occurred when we stained the deck to her condo together. It was backbreaking and grueling work but it was eased by simply being around a beautiful woman of God. In addition to everything else—she appeared to be incredibly supportive of my endeavors. God has blessed me with an opportunity to have my own radio show.

She was incredibly enthusiastic about it and help me secure my first guest for the show, who happened to be a close friend of hers. She would even assist me in the folding, and packaging of the bowties that I was selling. What more could I ever ask for from a woman? I had previously stated that I wouldn't date anyone with kids because I wasn't ready and mature enough to share. Due to the love that I had for her—I quickly changed my thinking and loved being around her daughter. When her daughter realized that I wasn't taking her mother away from her a bond was formed.

Her daughter was incredibly athletic, funny, smart and full of life. Our typically greeting consisted of me saying, "let me get some love from my favorite teen and giving her a hug. Despite the presence and involvement from her biological father—I was able to pick her up from school, swimming practice, and take her to dental visits. And I loved every minute of it. I even attempted to teach her how to drive in her school's parking lot and that was hilarious. I dropped my level of over-protectiveness and allowed my twins to hang out with my former friend without my presence. She would take them out and shop and they seemed to enjoy her company. They viewed her daughter as a big sister and wanted to emulate her, even to the point of getting their names on their book bags just like her. On several occasions, we hung all day as a "family" and enjoyed the movies, skating and ice cream.

With all of the love and quality time, the desire to be intimate grew stronger and stronger. I was trying to be obedient and remain celibate until marriage. It was something that I was practicing prior to meeting her. It was more difficult than I could imagine because I was madly in love with her. Eventually, we crossed the lines and the level of intimacy was better than expected. After moments of intimacy—we would look at each other and say in unison, *"God is not pleased and we are out of line."* Even in our sinful nature—I found a way to be in love with her because she feared God. I was impressed that she showed a level of contrition. At times, it was impossible to keep my hands off of her because she was so alluring and perfect in my eyes.

During her first birthday while we together—she did something that finalized (in my mind) she was the woman that I waited my whole life for. We were preparing to go out to brunch to celebrate her 48th. While she was in the shower—I snuck in all of her gifts and I was so happy at the thought of trying to make her happy. When she got out of the shower—she picked up a gift bag from a hidden place and handed it to me. I begin to laugh and said, *"do you realize it's your birthday and not mine?"* She got a gift for me on her birthday!! I found her gesture so loving, selfless, and amazing. In previous conversations—I told her that I would give my mate gifts on my birthday to let them know, even on my day, they are thought of and appreciated. It was as if she had literally transformed into everything that I desired.

Divine Interruption

Despite my current feeling of happiness—I wasn't naive enough to believe all the good times will continue to roll. In any relationship, the good times will be met with bad. During our two years, the love ebbed and flowed in periods of bliss and disharmony. My main issue in the heart of the relationship centered around her extreme eagerness to assist the church pastor with matters that were *absolutely* not church related. The late- night texts continued to plague us. There was definite altering of our relationship with this blatant interference.

I remember pleading with her on several occasions to let me know of any past dealings with him—sexual or otherwise. She would deny all of them and with each disavowal—I knew it was only a matter of time before I found out. Through a text message exchange from the two—I learned that he offered to pay for a plane ticket back to her home state after her grandmother passed. Initially, it seemed like a great gesture but I felt like it was the result of something deeper. I didn't say anything but I remember leaving her house immediately that evening. She was confused about my departure, but my emotion would not allow me to find the right words to convey. The hurt centered around the lack of trust she displayed with her secretive nature surrounding this man, but not his gesture in itself.

Most of our happy weekends were spent with each other going in and out of antique stores and thrift stores and dining out. One Saturday—we were scheduled to go out with our normal routine but she altered the plan. Walking towards the door, she paused saying, *"I'm caught in a dilemma."* Before I could reply and ask what dilemma she was referring to, she explained that she was caught up between the pastor of our church and *me*. She explained that he asked her come over to *his house* to do *his kids* hair. I was livid, feeling a new low point in our lives as she rarely offered to do my twin's hair. Her priorities were becoming clear to me as she proceeded to leave me to help him. I guess the fool in me didn't want to leave her house that night or leave the relationship for good. In hindsight—she had the best of both worlds. The attention and potential validation from a person she wanted; loyalty, dedication, and unconditional love from the person that absolutely wanted her. I had previously asked her to fully disclose any past intimate relationships in the church because I didn't want to jeopardize my worship experience. Her level of denial was high, but the stories became more convoluted raising my suspicions that something just not right. It felt like she would slip up and tell me things when I asked about the strangeness of their relationship.

Now that I can look at the situation with a different lens—I suspect she was telling me in her own way about their past sexual relationship, but I wanted to view it differently because I loved her. "*He was my friend while I went through a divorce and I would have never allowed him to come to my house because I would have been vulnerable and slept with him and had to wake up and repent.*" At this point, I was a licensed therapist and I couldn't understand why she would say such things, especially considering she would become enraged if she ever thought I was cheating on her. For example, I brought one of my colleagues to church to meet her because I thought she could serve as a mentor for her. After the service was over, she called me and without a greeting or warning demanding to know if I had known this woman in a biblical fashion. *"Did you used to sleep with this woman you brought to church?* She was extremely paranoid. She accused me of cheating when I would charge my phone within arm's reach of her without the need to even look at it. The confusing statements grew more and more. Within weeks of making these inflammatory statements—she had no recollection of them. She would report to me that this particular gentleman made statements to her in reference to losing weight, which describes the way she would impulsively spend hundreds of dollars on detox tea and other weight loss supplements.

After she accompanied a former minister at the church (friend of hers) to a contentious meeting with the Pastor, as her friend was departing on bad terms, due to a perceived slight. When the meeting was over—she told me that he responded to them by saying, *"you can't come to my office and talk to me like I slept with you last night."* The other minister told her *"girl if he could sleep with you, he would."* On numerous occasions—the writing was on the wall. For instance, we were having Christmas dinner at the aforementioned friend's house. The fellowship and food were good until her friend's boyfriend and I started watching the basketball game on TV. He was making comments that led me to believe that he was trying to tell me something. I was so caught up in the delicious food that I was not really comprehending. He asked me to step out on the porch so others in the house, who were still members of the church couldn't hear. He told me that some things are church-related and should be done in the church and not in the Pastor's home. He was referring to everything from her going to his house to doing the kids hair. I didn't attempt to get in a word because he was on a roll. God was telling me that this situation isn't right but the blinders were on me and I couldn't see what was being done and or said. My demeanor, mindset, and the overall mood shifted the rest of the evening. She noticed the difference in me. I put myself through the mental anguish and doing the ride back to her house I asked again, and she denied it again.

With every attempt to help her, she would say "*you are never there for me.*" Her words and actions were now impossible to understand. It was times that I felt like I was dealing with two different people. Instead of be pushed away from her—I became more attracted and tried harder to please her. It was a draining toll taken on me, because it felt like my efforts were never enough; while her attempts to do anything in our relationship for me—stopped completely. Some weeks—she needed me to be there to comfort and cuddle, and other weeks—she would distance herself greatly. It can best be described as, "*I Hate You!*" but, "*Don't Leave Me.*" I remember receiving a raging phone call ordering me to come get my spare set of clothes "*the hell out*" of her house. Only weeks later, this same woman was encouraging me to keep my clothes at her house—so I could stay.

In those moments—I didn't know what I could have done to provoke it. I was being pushed and pulled in multiple directions. The down feeling of being trapped in a winless situation weighed on my spirit heavily. On one occasion—she stated, "*it's me and not you—I want space,*" and I walked to the door to oblige her. She grabbed my hand and said, "*Don't go.*" A *Catch 22* situation had devolved further into a living nightmare. My dream woman was now gone. She was critical about the way I dressed. I have never been the recipient of a woman being that verbally abusive towards me. I think back now that maybe some of her thoughts about her own self-consciousness were being projected onto me. As a result of this—she would put down all of my dreams, my desires to rise as a speaker and future author. She belittled all of my aspirations. I often wondered if the statements of insecurity were a reflection of herself and an attempt to get me to stay because I won't have the confidence to succeed in another relationship.

At the time, I think it was working. I was constantly questioning everything about myself; my strong foundation had been chipped, no—jackhammered down from its strongest point. I even had doubts about my calling from God. Low was not even a good enough descriptor where I was.

I recall sharing with her the vision that God wanted me to minister his Word and of course; I was expecting a favorable response. The vision frightened me because it made me question my mental health. For a period of one month; I began to see my face on the Pastor's body during the Sunday service. The image was so vivid that I stopped looking at him during the sermons. When I told her, she replied, "M*aybe God is giving you an idea of what not to do when you are in the position of leading the church.*" It was as if she was frightened by the very thought of *me* being *successful.* I always emphasize that if I'm successful, so are you. I thought our relationship would have been strengthening as ministers and lovers. Another instance was the college. Mentioning any college, and specifically, that I graduated from college was a big no-no. It was the starting point for World War III. Apparently, not completing college was a challenge she had previously experienced. I contacted one of the local colleges and got brochures sent to her house to show my level of care and concern and to galvanize her because I knew how much it meant to her. This gesture was not taken lightly and I was criticized for it. Despite what she believed—I made a daily effort to let her know of her beauty and her worth—but I don't think I was ever successful. On many sleepless nights, my heart ached due to a lack of self-love she possessed. For an individual who had battled self-love issues—I was able to give her the effort to love herself more than I have ever given myself. I often believed and told her that when she found her purpose, life will be so much better.

We considered multiple options like trying to get an assisted living facility, selling detox tea, t-shirts and starting her dream of owning an in-home daycare. I remember passing out promotional fliers for her daycare in a blinding snowstorm. Her response was, "*If you really loved me—you would've passed all of them out*." She had projects that were still in the dream phase. I tried to assist where I could, but to no avail. I was beginning to pay more attention to her behaviors but couldn't figure out what was going on. Her sense of self-changed from week to week, even with her attire. She would impulsively shop and they want to buy even newer clothes to change her look. For example, she pur-chased a pair of women's sneakers that I mentioned would look good on her. During one outburst—she yelled at me about *making* her buy sneakers. "*I only bought them to keep you happy*." It was very strange to me because my love for her wasn't based on anything but her.

The arguments were more frequent in nature and the honeymoon period were gone. My methodology of handling the conflict never made the situations better. I was under the false impression that I could solve all our problems by talking them out without properly processing everything. This was one of the worst strategies. Due to the nature of my profession, I know the power that exists in therapy. So quite naturally, I suggested we try therapy. With that, she became more defensive and angrier than I have ever seen. I would later understand the meaning of her reaction. On one particular night, she was sitting on the edge of her bed, deep in thought. I could see something was bothering her and I was careful about asking anything, trying to avoid more conflict. She mentioned that her sister was diagnosed and suffering from bipolar disorder. I walked over and hugged her because I understood the impact of mental health as a client and as a therapist. She said I was the first person that she ever told.

I expressed my feelings about it, which of course, let her know it doesn't define a person and that help is available. From a therapeutic perspective—I offered to help as much as possible. I would later question myself and wonder if this was her way of trying to reveal the challenge she was facing. It was incredibly painful to think I missed a potential opportunity to help someone I was in love with. This thought and the possibilities of what I could have changed—has walked the corridors of my mind haunting me—for quite some time.

Despite all of the challenges we faced—we remained together and I had hopes for the future. However, that same hope for the future started to drastically change around March 2018. She was informed that she was being laid off from her job. I felt bad for her and helped as much as possible. On March 29, 2018, we had an argument about her inability to show me the same level of care and concern that I had always shown to her. Earlier in the day, I expressed that my grandmother was hospitalized. To be honest—I was expecting her to reach out and be the supportive partner that I once fell in love with. Looking back at it now—I blame myself for having that expectation of someone else, even someone in relationship with me.

It was one of those situations in my life where I focused my thinking on the following; Psalm 84:12 *Lord Almighty, blessed is the one who trusts in you.* (NIV) I was trusting in a woman to do something only God could do, which was providing peace in my heart and my mind regarding my grandmother's health. The next day was Good Friday and I tried to make peace with the previous days' issues—but we weren't able to communicate effectively—which was normal for us. We walked past each other in church and didn't speak. It was an awkward feeling. Later that night, I ran out of gas while working my part-time job. I called her with the thought she would make an attempt to help me out, but that backfired. She advised me that I did something crazy and didn't speak to her in the church. She hung up the phone and refused to answer again. As a result of this—I allowed my anger to cloud my better judgment and make a few idiotic decisions that would change the very course of my life. First, after putting gas in my car—I drove to her house. I was driving with the intention of talking about why she (or so I felt) made no effort to assist me. I should have used some of the skills that I teach to my clients. Deeply in the point of anger—I should've realized that nothing positive was going to take place. In addition to this—I should have considered that her communication in such a state of mind was probably going to not end well between us. She was an individual who liked to process before commenting or reacting to a situation. Me, on the other hand, I like to discuss it immediately and not have stress about when the conversation would occur.

Arriving at her house—I saw her looking out of the window at me. She then cut out the lights and that hurt me more than her not coming to get me. For a man—it was more damaging to my pride to think she doesn't care in the same regard that I do. Perhaps it triggered some latent abandonment issues that I never dealt with. Maybe I was jumping to an unnecessary conclusion. In the world of therapy, I would refer to it as a cognitive distortion. I knocked on the door—already knowing what the response would be. Then I proceeded to kick the door twice to further express my frustration.

When I got in my car—I thought what did I do? I quickly realized that it wasn't a good decision and I wasn't sure how my life would be impacted as a result of it. Secondly, in my eagerness to vent my frustration—I called her about 50 times between Friday and Saturday night. At that moment, I could justify my selfish actions. The following day, I called her and I heard a voice ask her the following question, *"what is his date of birth?"* I was puzzled by the strangeness of the question. For some reason, my intuition kicked in and I drove past the police station in her neighborhood. Doing a previous argument—she had threatened me with the police before. As I drove past the police station—I saw her car and as I got out of my car—I saw her walking out. I said, *"hey, what is going on and can I talk to you?"* She ran inside the police station as if I was chasing her. The officer at the precinct was literally screaming at me to leave. I proceeded to leave, got in my car and pulled off in haste. The lack of control with my emotions led me to believe I could still get *"my point"* across. This was my fault; my logic in thought was nowhere to be found. I pulled up next to her and said again. *"can we talk?"* As she begins to utter a few words—I saw two police officers rushing to my car. I was immediately yanked out of my car and arrested for trespassing on government property, telephone misuse, and failure to obey a reasonable and lawful order.

WHAT HAS JUST HAPPENED? I know what happened but I really couldn't process what happened. I was subsequently processed at the precinct and taken to another facility in order to be released. During my 12-hour detainment, I was getting impatient and I heard my name called on several occasions. I was informed by one of the officers that the holdup is getting the protective order paperwork. Did I think about a protective order? She filed a protective order against me which prohibited any contact to be made to her. After my release—I was given my belongings, which included my phone and I immediately called one of her friends to see what in the world had just happened. Her friend offered me the following words, *"give her some space and if she wants to call you—she will. I'm sure she has your number."* I caught a bus back to my car, which was still parked in front of the police station. Luckily for me, it wasn't towed away.

When I got home, I frantically explained this to my mother. At my request, I asked my mom to call her on my behalf to see if she was okay and attempt to gain an idea of what happened. That didn't work out so well and ended in a very short phone call. On Easter Sunday—I got a call from my friend who introduced us and she said, *"please, tell me that it isn't so."* Then she asked the question. *"Do you know she called the church and said she isn't coming back if you come."* My mouth dropped, along with my heart. She continued by saying—she told the security team that she doesn't know me. What do you mean? Apparently—my former friend led the security team to believe that she never knew me at all and I was a random guy. Sure, breakups are bad, but to mention that you didn't know me. This was bizarre, to say the least!

Luckily, my friend that introduced us was able to give the truth about our two-year relationship. This was turning into more of a biblical story by the minute. I would equate this to Peter denying Jesus on more than occasion. It was one of the most painful things that I have heard in my life. I was in total shock. She had no remembrance of me at all? That is impossible considering we were a couple. Can someone just turn off a switch and forget you? This situation was getting more and more interesting by the minute. Once again, I knew something wrong but I didn't know what exactly. Along with the other emotions that were at the forefront of my brain pounding on me continuously—a deep sadness became one of the central ones that I would feel quite often.

The following business day from my arrest—we appeared in court for the peace order hearing. She arrived in court with a familiar person, one of her friends in ministry who was the first guest on my radio show. The judge was no-nonsense, quick to interrupt others, including lawyers and defendants alike type of person. His tongue was sharper than a sword, as he cut people in half with some of his words. As my case was heard—she encouraged the judge to bar me from returning to the church. He quickly denied her requesting stating that it would be unfair to deny a man to the opportunity to worship freely. Prior to proceeding forward, he asked her if the relationship was over, and she took a long pause and said yes. He felt like we should be able to worship in the church without further incident.

So, for the next two months—we attended the same church. I was under the impression that I could still receive the word of God, despite seeing and being near an individual whom at the moment we were experiencing major problems with each other. On many Sunday mornings—we would inadvertently make eye contact and those beautiful eyes that I used to desire with such a lovingkindness, caused me to look away. Her eyes used to say *"Rashad, I love you,"* but at the present moment, it was more like *"I can't stand you."* It was an awful experience but I made an attempt to push through it all. It was taking a heavy toll on me. There were two moments that caused me to leave the church with the goal of never returning.

I was at work finishing my lesson, as I was teaching adult Sunday school every third week. I received a call and I was informed that I couldn't teach Sunday School to until a decision is made in court. This happened to be a direct attempt from her to bury me. It was a dagger in my heart because I fell in love with learning, teaching, and sharing the word of God. A large point of the sting is that the decision was made without any attempt to hear my side of the story. The second disheartening moment was learning (through several trusted sources) that my friend lied to me constantly about her past and possible ongoing sexual relationship with the gentlemen of the church. All of my fears had been confirmed. I would often ruminate on the *I should've, would've, could've* thoughts in an effort to try and cope. I felt betrayed because I came into the relationship with the intent of being completely honest. *And I was.*

It was getting worse before it got better because the Pastor was throwing shots at me from the pulpit. He mentioned that his ministers should have discernment before getting involved with idiots. I'm inclined to believe these comments were made prior to all of the details surfacing and they were based on her description of me. I think he and I were both caught up in some altered version of Eric Benet's hit song *Hurricane*. Swirling in the heavy tempest—to at least *one* of our dooms.

My next plight was a scheduled a meeting with Pastor to get some answers about being sat down from teaching Sunday school. Many of my beloved inner circle of friends advised me against going to the meeting because I was still emotionally invested in her. The meeting could have gone two drastically different ways. It could have produced a level of closure in my mind or it could it have been more damaging to learn more lies and deceit at the expense of my mental health. About a week before the meeting—I decided not to go. Despite the enormous level of betrayal experienced—I still had her best interest at heart. I know that the potential existed for her to be asked to step down from her position, but that wasn't my goal. It honestly felt like church was the place to hide her mental illness, whether she was aware of it or not—but it was not my place to seek her ruination. I was still trying to operate from a place of love in the presence of duplicity.

In my final departing from the parish, I decided to go into church for the final time to give my Sunday school family thank-you cards. They were instrumental in my learning the word of God—and for that—I am eternally grateful. In addition to this, they encouraged me to teach and saw something in me that I did not see in myself. The energy in the church was odd on that final Sunday for me because I felt like everyone was looking at me. I learned that her whispering campaign to the security team failed as her lies were revealed. Clarity had shown me that she hid our relationship so well that no one in the church knew with the exception of a few people.

She was crafty in creating a narrative for everyone that I had an issue with the Pastor, which wasn't the issue at all. I guess I would be more dastardly evil in other people's eyes if I was considered a threat to him. It was actually my hurt and frustration with her actions that angered me to that low, sad place I mentioned earlier. I allowed that emotive measure in me to manifest in a lack of respect in God's house, which is one of my greatest regrets. I remember bringing a book to church at one point and reading it as I paid no attention to the Pastor or his message. My level of petty turned into self-righteous protest in the most inappropriate of arenas.

Someone would later tell me that my face was like a prizefighter when he walked to the ring. I had to ask God for forgiveness for entering his house angry and operating from a place of pure, raw emotion.

One of his armor-bearers, who I know, and consider a good guy and spoke with on a regular basis during this situation, was giving me a look—as if to say—*we have to fight*. His reaction was based on the stories and information she was providing. I couldn't believe this was happening, especially not in a church. During this time, my mental health was at an all-time low. I was dealing with depression and anxiety that caused me to look like a walking, talking zombie. I was sleeping two hours a night with an incredible sense of worry. I was drowning myself with all the wrong comforts like soda, cookies, ice cream, and sleeping medications just to cope on a daily basis. All of the mental health experience and training that I had was not working *for me*.

One of my colleagues, who is an amazing mental health expert called me over to her desk. This didn't surprise me at all because we had these heart-to-heart conversations every Monday. We would share stories about a variety of topics and I would often express how proud how I was of her—as she was pursuing her Ph.D. She suggested I have been thinking about your situation and want you to read a few articles on a variety of mental health challenges. She suggested that I read these articles and further educate myself on bipolar and borderline personality. She said many of the symptoms that your ex-friend displayed were extremely consistent with the borderline personality disorder. The constant fear of abandonment, self-induced instability, mood swings, depression, impulsive behaviors, paranoia, and social isolation—were a few symptoms. Each day, I would immerse myself in reading on the disorder. Article after article, eventually moving on to books. I begin to replay countless moments in my head in where I would've reacted differently if I knew what she may have been enduring. It is important to note too that I'm unaware if she was ever official diagnosed. I begin to beat myself up by not being able to detect the challenges she was facing. It led me to question my level of therapeutic expertise. The situation with my new learning was so hard for me to process how could I have missed opportunities to help someone that I was in truly love with. This haunted for a long time. I even questioned God asking him if was this an assignment that I messed up.

I started to keep my Bible near my bed and if I woke up in the middle of the night (which happened often) I would read and recite the following verse multiple times. **Matthew 11:28**, *Come to me, all you who are weary and burdened, and I will give you rest* (NIV) With time pressing forward, some days and nights were slightly better than others. Even if I thought I might be experiencing a moment of peace—reality was constant in reminding me otherwise. One of the pastor's close relatives, who probably in his 90's and reminded me of my grandfather— inquired about my absence from Sunday school. I was done with everything that was church related at this point. Quite frankly, I couldn't even imagine walking into a church in the near future. However, my respect and love for him were too high to ignore. He summoned me to his house to discuss my absence. He possessed an infinite amount of wit, knowledge, and a wise love for God. His words were so powerful and when he talked, even with his seasoned elder tone, it was piercing and you had no choice but to listen.

When I arrived at his house, which was located in a historic community, I walked up the steps, knocking and he beckoned for me to come on in. He was sitting with his legs crossed in the kitchen. He got up slowly and directed me to his living room. After my really long explanation about what happened, I wondered what wisdom would be dropped on me. He smiled, paused, and I knew he was about to tell me something profound. I was on the edge of my seat at this point, waiting in anticipation. He said, "*it sounds like you were a pawn in the game she was playing.*" I was extremely confused and told him that I need clarity. He said, "*pawns in a chess game are manipulated in an expendable manner.*" He illustrated further by saying, "*she used you to see if the pastor would be jealous and want her.*" He laughed again, and I said, I don't think that was the case. I could not see anything clearly as my love for her clouded my emotions and thinking.

My head couldn't take all of the information that he provided me. I was truly overwhelmed. One of the things that I will never forget from this conversation was his words to never stop loving and trusting God. To be honest—he was extremely adamant for me to continue searching for a church home. He extended himself to me if I needed to talk and pray. I left his house, even more, damaged and crestfallen than before. *Did she have this plan in place all along? Was she just a cold and emotionless person only concerned with her own wellbeing?* In the following weeks—I mentally thought about attending a church. For the next few weeks—I would use Sunday morning to get extra sleep. I stopped opening my Bible and everything about church sickened me. If I heard church music on the radio—I was quickly turning the station. My prayer life diminished so tremendously that when I decided to pray, it was short, meaningless and felt forced.

Eventually—I decided to give the church a try again and I went to a church near my house. When I got out of my car—one of the deacons from across the parking lot, said, *Welcome!* Before I could return the greeting, he said, *"Son, are you okay?"* I can only assume that I looked stressed. I replied thanks for the welcome and I'm just fine, all of which was a huge lie. As I entered the church, I immediately reminisced about my former church and felt uncomfortable. When I sat down, I was delighted by the sound of the choir and felt joyous. Then, I mentally collapsed. I felt one tear starting to form and then I put my head down. The stream followed afterward to the point that my shirt and jacket were soaked. Some of the ministers walked over to me and placed their hands on me and prayed so hard. I never got an opportunity to see their faces because I did not have the strength to pick my head up. I imagine my head was buried for quite some time. When I finally stop crying, I got up and walked out. I headed home, ripped off my clothes and attempted to sleep the rest of the day away. No more church for me!

Many of my sleepless nights were filled with thoughts about the previous good times in which I felt like I was experiencing a love straight out of heaven. Part of my faulty thinking led me to believe we would overcome this and be together. As the court date quickly approached—I was certain that the outcome would be favorable because the charges were misdemeanors and I thought the contentious nature of our relationship was over.

The Courtroom

"Trust in the Lord with your heart and lean not on your own understanding." **Proverbs 3:5 (NKJV)**

Despite the amount of stress that I was under, I continued to work hard to advance my professional life forward. My summer was booked with speaking and other professional engagements that were aligned with my purpose. June 18—was one of those days where I was able to combine many of my passions. Walking into the Baltimore City Juvenile Justice Center where I had been employed for the last three years as a licensed clinical professional counselor—helped me walk in my purpose. I was responsible for conducting individual and group therapy with young men who have been detained on a variety of charges. This particular Monday wasn't different from any other Monday. Before I could make my way to the unit, I had to stop at the thick metal door, hit the buzzer, and wait for someone inside the master control bubble to grant me access. I would always stop and wonder, *why* would people allow themselves to be in a position where you have little or no control of your freedom? If for some reason, it took longer than I wanted for them to open the door, my lack of patience would take over and I would be instantly frustrated. The frustration would stem from not being accustomed to waiting on something as simple as the opening of a door.

I never got used to the sound of the door slamming behind me. Even though I wasn't an inmate—it was ever present reminder that I was in jail. Thankfully, I was always able to leave whenever I wanted to.

After completing the group for that day—I raced out of the building and headed towards one of the largest hotels in Maryland. I was afforded the opportunity to present my public speaking course to a major organization. My presentation was on two large screens inside of a huge conference room. I was on a natural high. As speaker and presenter—I always give each opportunity my all. I knew each opportunity could positively impact others and I realized that at any time—I might not be able to do what I loved to do. After the event had concluded, I got in my car, opened the sunroof and increased the volume on Jay-Z's and Beyoncé song, *"Nice."* I repeatedly said, *"blessing on blessing...feeling like best year ever."* I fought the rush hour traffic back to Baltimore just in time for my twins first swimming practice. All of the stars were aligning for me. Little did I know; this was the calm before the storm.

I arrived at the courthouse in typical *Rashad Mills Style*, which meant I was there well in advance. In this case, I was outside in the parking lot approximately 1 hour and 15 minutes earlier than what I needed to be. As I sat in my car, sipping on my coffee reflecting on what was about to happen, I wasn't too worried about the outcome. As I got out and headed to the elevator—I saw a young lady who resembled my former friend. She had the build, attire, and walk of my friend. But I was immediately drawn to the briefcase that she in her hand. My initial reaction told me that she printed the phone records. Maybe I jumping to unnecessary conclusions. For some reason, my calmness quickly evaporated and my anxiety took over. After walking into the courthouse and going through the scanner—I looked around for my public defender to discuss the matter briefly before heading into court. He had previously assured me through our phone conversations that the judge would have bigger fish to fry than worry about my misdemeanor case. Additionally, he had spoken with the state's attorney who mentioned that he had no desire to pursue jail time. I wanted to resolve this case and move on as quickly as possible. Once I located my public defender—he informed that the presiding judge was a sarcastic but fair man.

He even asked me if I had thought about postponing the case, which I quickly denied. I sat outside of the courtroom and I noticed that my former friend was walking into the courthouse. The walk that I was once happy to see, appeared to be a walk of doom for me she was accompanied by her daughter. That was extremely odd because most parents want to shed their kids from the potential harm of courtrooms. Her 14-year old daughter was not a part of the case and I began thinking that she wanted to use her daughter as a witness because her daughter was in the house when I acted out. Could a young lady, who loved I like one of my daughters and I thought the world of—be called to take the stand against me?

Maybe she wanted to sway the judge with the goal of putting me in a bad situation by bringing her daughter. I couldn't think of the reasons behind it. This was not her typical mode of operation. Was someone else driving this behavior? While inside of the courtroom, I stood in line and checked in the with the state's attorney. I happen to look up and I saw the same judge who handled the previous protective order case. My friend noticed I was in line and intentionally got up and walked past me. I was becoming more and more uneasy about the outcome. I felt that her energy was coming from a vengeful place. Just a month and a half prior, I was entering a coffee house that we both would frequent, and I saw her truck outside. Due to the contentious nature of our relationship—I didn't dare look in her direction because I was afraid of her reaction. My phone becomes the distraction that I needed to avoid looking in her direction. She waited outside until I ordered my coffee and then I saw her pull off. Was she aiming to get back at me for a perceived abandonment? All of my imagined propositions seemed damming to my plight for an easy outcome of this hearing.

My goal was to sit in front of the courtroom to avoid any possible eye contact. I sat in the front row in the farthest corner possible. As I listened to all of the cases before me—I was getting restless and I rested my head in my lap. Then I sat up and used my hand as a blinder to avoid any chance of us looking at each other. I glanced at my watch and over two hours had elapsed. Finally, my case had been called. My public defender and the state attorneys stated their cases and I thought I was ready to put to an end this nightmarish situation. The case was running as smoothly as I had originally planned. The judge learned of my profession as a therapist and he informed me that he had inmates in lockup that needed mental health services. I replied for the right price that I would assist them. The courts, along with him found it pretty funny.

My mother always told me that my mouth would get me in trouble one day. As a therapist—I'm keenly aware of the importance of trying to get closure in relationships. I wanted to gain a sense of closure by simply apologizing in an environment where my words and actions wouldn't get misinterpreted. Despite how the relationship ended, I wanted to let her know that I didn't harbor any hate or malice towards her. My public defender asked the judge for his permission and he granted it. She was positioned behind me so my better judgment told me not to turn around and look at her, but look directly at the judge. I expressed a heartfelt apology to her but I was looking at the judge. The state's attorney got up in a rage and stated that if my apology was sincere—I would have looked directly looked at my ex-friend. Out of the blue—he stated she wants nothing to do with your honor. It was an unexpected shift in his demeanor. The judge stated that he didn't have an issue with my apology and mentioned that he understood why I didn't turn around and look at her. The state attorney quickly shifted from docile to Doberman pinscher. He encouraged my ex-friend to give a statement about me and it wasn't favorable.

I felt like she was out to get back at me. Up until this point—I had dated her several years—and never saw a tear flow, but now, from some well I had never seen—she was filled with tearful emotions that I had on no occasion, ever witnessed. I could hear a plethora of emotions from her. She was throwing well-placed verbal darts—and apparently—they all landed on the target she was aiming for. That target appeared to be the emotional strings of the judge's heart. This was the beginning of my ending. The judge looked down as if he was looking at some notes and he when he picked his head up—the course of my life would be forever changed when he mentioned the following:

Mr. Mills, after hearing the testimony of this young lady, I look at you differently despite all of the work you do in the community as a motivational speaker, the therapist at a jail, and an upstanding man of the community. Under the sentencing guidelines—I sentence you to three years in jail with two and a half years suspended and three years of probation.

(All of sudden, time slowed down enough for me to think) that his next words would be, you will be on probation for six months or maybe probation before judgment. BOY, I WAS WRONG!!!

BAILIFF, CUFF HIM. My public defender countered with an attempt to get an appeal bond, which was subsequently denied. Was *Rashad Mills* really on his way to The Baltimore County Detention Center? AKA *JAIL?* I was in a state of shock as my body went completely numb. I was handcuffed walking down to the elevator to be taken to a holding cell. I felt like I was in a *Spike Lee Joint* walking in scene alone; all the focus and weight of the world upon me. Strangely enough, I was able to process the following thought: *God, I trust you but what about my kids, my job, my house, my car, my life?* I knew I was trusting *in* God but I didn't have any idea of what I was trusting him *for.*

Prior to being placed in the holding cell—I had my first of many encounters, with a correctional officer who didn't care at all about *Rashad "Bowtie" Mills.* He was responsible for taking my belongings like shoe strings to prevent suicide, my watch, and other possessions that are not allowed in the jailhouse. He was curt, emotionless and treated me just like the rest of the inmates. In the following moments— I learned two very important things; that I wasn't important, like at all. I also learned you will become more accomplished with humility and kindness as opposed to arrogance. My ego led me to believe that he was aware that I was an up and coming motivational speaker, radio host, therapist, and a man of God. Maybe he should have treated me with more respect. I wanted to match his level of nastiness but I decided to do something differently. It wasn't his fault that I was detained. He allowed me to make a phone call to Will and he was able to get my phone and other important items.

As I sat in the holding cell—I said to myself this isn't how my day was supposed to pan out. Truthfully, I was planning to purchase a new phone, get some coffee and prepare for my weekly radio show. The other guys/detainees in the cell gave me a puzzling look. I could feel their eyes looking at me and I was preparing for my first jail fight because they probably sensed I was soft because I didn't fit the typical jail look, if anything, even exists. Keep in mind, I was dressed in my normal attire which consists of dress slacks, dress shirt, slippery earls (dress shoes), and my signature piece, a bowtie. The ice was finally broken when I was asked, *"dude, why are you here?"* I hesitated for a second and shared the story. The reaction from both of the young men was the same. *WHAT IN THE HELL IS THAT CHARGE? AND YOU GOT HOW MUCH TIME FOR THAT?* I was charged with telephone misuse or excessive calls.

They immediately begin to give me a false sense of hope. As I later would find out, the majority of inmates are skilled at being jailhouse lawyers. I heard a plethora of phrases like *"you will be out of here in no time,"* and *"they made a mistake by doing that to you."* Within the hour that we sat in a dirty cell that had writing on the wall that was equivalent to a middle school boys' bathroom. I listened to everyone talks about their individual stories that landed them in the "*big house.*" Many of the stories included handguns, drugs, gang affiliation, and shockingly enough—the possibility of bail. Once again, I began to question the legal system that I was detained on a misdemeanor where no one was physically hurt—but I accepted my wrongdoings.

Prior to my detainment, I was a listened mental health therapist at the Baltimore City Juvenile Justice Center. Interestingly enough, about two weeks before my arrest—I completed a group with the young man about good choices and not placing yourself in a position to be arrested or re-arrested. Apparently, I didn't listen to my own advice. *Who knew* how fast my life would change? I was asking myself the same questions. One of the early realities that jail life was dramatically different from civilian life was the unassuming task of using the bathroom. Something so simple as using the bathroom hit me like a ton of bricks.

Now, by all accounts, I have been referred to a guy that takes good care of himself, which for me included manicures, pedicures, good colognes and etc. In addition to this, I would like to use the bathroom in peace often accompanied with a little music, maybe a candle and maybe a good book for my reading pleasure. As I stood over the toilet—I heard my mother's voice, "*you need to clean the toilet and sink because this is unacceptable.*" I believe the sink and toilet were supposed to have a shiny silverfish color, but this one was a dingy black and looked as if no one should ever touch it. I wasn't terrified, but I knew that this would be my life for the next 6 months. I managed to use the bathroom and to be honest—I couldn't even wash my hands due to the lack of soap. Water had to do.

The immediate stress of the situation seemed to drain my battery and I found myself dozing off to sleep. When in Rome, do as the Romans do. This old adage applies to a multitude of situations in life, especially in jail. I knew this would be an extremely difficult process to attempt to find any level of comfort in. So, I pressed my back against the cold, concrete wall and begin to fall asleep. I have no idea how long was I asleep, but I was awakened to the following shout, *Alright, Fellas, let's roll out*. I woke up and thought it was a dream and my "normal" life would resume. The nightmare was just beginning.

Processing

"And Jesus said to them, "I am the bread of life. He who comes to Me shall never hunger, and he who believes in Me shall never thirst.""
John 6:35 (NKJV)

After a ride to the Baltimore County Detention Center in luxury transportation dis-affectionately known as the paddy wagon, I was officially processed. I never knew the excess of tests and questions that an inmate is subject to. I was pissed off so I was short and direct with all of my answers. *"Rashad, have you ever"* and before they could finish- the answer was *NO!!!* It was all too familiar for me because I had to ask some of the same questions to the young men that I worked with at the juvenile facility.

Since Baltimore is relatively small—I began to wonder if I would notice anyone that I knew. Due to the unexpected nature of my detainment, I was still afraid of my image and how I would be perceived as an inmate. Let's face it—a large portion of society is not very caring towards people that have been incarcerated. I was called to the front desk for another round of questions and to take my photo which would be my identification for my jail ID bracelet. The thick, ugly, yellow bracelet officialized that I was *inmate 458627*. It's a number that I will never forget for the rest of my life—as God gives me strength. The gentlemen at the front desk had an easy disposition about him and he could see I was visibly shaken about being detained. While he was inputting information in the computer- I randomly mentioned that my shock was resulting from the fact that yesterday I was working in a juvenile jail and now I'm an inmate in jail. He looked up at me with a concerning look and I said, *"What's wrong?"* He told me to on hold for a minute while he talked to his supervisor to get clarification on a few things. He came back and asked me if I wanted to be housed in the PC unit. PC? From where I come from PC is short for protective custody and that's a very low level of street credibility.

He told me that it wasn't mandatory but I did have the option for safety and security purposes. I guess he was concerned that I may encounter a juvenile that I previously worked with that may want to do harm to me. I kind of laughed at that notion because I treated the young men that I worked with the same level of care, kindness, and love that I did with my own kids. In addition to that—I wouldn't allow my manhood to be reduced to protective custody. Although I would never be mistaken for a UFC fighter or *Iron Mike Tyson*—I was more than capable of handling myself in any situation. For a hazy moment in time—

I thought my mind was playing tricks on me as I thought I heard my name being repeatedly called. I looked straight ahead and didn't recognize the inmates; however, I was still hearing my name being called repeatedly. Ready to face whatever it was, I turned around and saw a somewhat familiar face. This face was contorted at a unique angle (between the cell door) to allow his voice to be heard, *"Mr. Mills, Mr. Mills, what's up good brother?"* I instantly recognized the voice and the face as one of the young men that I had worked with at the Baltimore City Juvenile Justice Center. He said, *"Mr. Mills what in the devil's hell are you doing here?"* He thought I was providing mental health services to inmates until I flashed my newest piece of jewelry, which was my inmate ID bracelet. He gave me a sad look and then uttered the words, *DAMN MR. MILLS*. I thanked him for his kind words and concern. Without going blank, I instinctively went into therapist mode by becoming an active listener as he told me his reason for being detained. I found myself in a particularly interesting situation because I was trying to assist someone else, but yet, I am in need of assistance myself. Emotionally, I was in a ball of tears on the inside but I refused to show it. It had to be one of the most humbling experiences in my life. Little did I know, there would be many more to come.

After being screened by the medical and mental health departments- I had to sit in an area known as the PIT. It was fitting because you are sitting below everyone else. After a conversation upon my release with a sister in Christ—I would learn that the PIT is an acronym for place intended for the transition. I walked up and down the steps from the PIT multiple times to use the telephone. Due to the numbers being memorized in my phone, I could only remember one number and that was to my brother William Rodgers.

In a span of a few hours, I probably called it for what seems like a few hundred times. He was what a brother should be in a time of absolute turmoil. He was calm and vowed to help me as much as possible until I was a free man. I begin to hear a loud rumbling and thought my mind was playing tricks on me. It was my stomach and I realized that I hadn't eaten all day. The coffee that I had earlier in the morning was satisfying but couldn't count as a meal. Lucky for me—it was lunchtime. The lunch wasn't the equal portions of protein, carbohydrates, and vegetables that I was used to. It came in the form of a beige paper bag and the surprise was inside. This was the first opportunity, although I declined it, to meet *Sweaty Betty*. Please be mindful that *Betty* is not an actual woman but the name of the bologna sandwich which is served in jail and prisons. It was slimy and reeked of a foul odor that I couldn't accurately describe any known origin. It was wrapped in a plastic that required the strength of Samson to rip open. The cheese was discolored and I refused to allow myself to eat anything that came out of that paper bag. Well, I did eat the potato chips and the pre-packaged cookies. At this point, I was only detained for about 4-6 hours and I was already wondering how was I going to survive on this food.

Receiving

"Yea, though I walk through the valley of the shadow of death,
I will fear no evil; For You are with me; Your rod and Your staff,
they comfort me." **Psalm 23 (NJKV)**

After completing the intake process, I was placed into another cell, which is the normal process when in jail. It is the ultimate lesson in patience and I believe it's done intentionally to get you accumulated to functioning on someone else's time. God knows I struggled with patience and I believed he used this as a teaching moment. The shock and disbelief are now creeping in my mind at a much higher rate. Is this a game? Is this real? Will something happen so that I will get out in a few hours? All of these questions and thoughts ran marathon-sized laps in my mind.

After sitting in the cell for hours, we were let out and walked about 100 feet and stopped in front of an area that resembled a bathroom. The guard said, *"Mills, step up and walk into one of the corners and strip naked before you get your new uniform."* *Strip naked??* Maybe, it took me longer than normal to process what was said because he said, *"Mills, did you hear me?"* I heard him but my brain was operating on a delay. I undressed in a corner, then I had to do something that totally degraded me as a person, and a man. I had to cough and swat. Cough and swat are a term used by law enforcement, particularly inside of jail and detention centers to make sure that inmates don't have any illegal items on or inside of them. I was in my birthday suit, in front of a grown man. It was first of many—totally degrading experiences as an inmate. After a few minutes—my wardrobe changed from dress clothes to an over-sized yellow jumper. I was given a pair of shoes that resembled karate attire. They were navy blue and had no sole or support. It was the equivalent of walking around with nothing on your feet. The jumper was big enough for three people to fit in it. I was given a net bag that contained the following items: toothbrush, toothpaste, toilet paper, spork, and a burgundy plastic cup.

After sitting in another cell for a few more hours—I finally got to stretch my legs as I walked to my home for the next four or five days, which was the receiving area. All of the jail shows that I watched had prepared me to walk on a unit as the new inmate. The other inmates stop and stared as if they hadn't seen humans before. I truly understand the psychology behind it all. They were probably doing the same thing I was doing to them which was sizing them up. One of the first things that struck me as odd, was the location of the guards. They were located in a bubble and not in the immediate area with the inmates. If something happened—someone could've died or been seriously hurt prior to help ever arriving.

The second thing that struck me as odd was the number of inmates in such a small area. I quickly glanced around and thought there were more inmates than places to sleep. And I was correct. When I stepped in the unit, I was literally stepping over other guys. There were laying in what are referred to as boats. The plastically shaped sleeping beds are shaped in a boat like fashion. Fortunately for me—I only had to sleep on it for one night. It wasn't pleasing to the neck and back, and it wasn't comfortable for the mind. For my first official night in jail, I had to keep one eye open because I was uncertain of the culture that I was now a part of. I was eventually given a better sleeping option: the top bunk. Although I was familiar with bunk beds as a child—this was far from the pristine wooden bunk beds that my brother and I slept in as kids. As an inmate, I quickly realized that everything must be viewed from a new, relative lens. My bunk was a thin piece of steel paired with the little sheet that barely covered half of my body. It was a huge upgrade from the boat, so there wasn't a need to complain.

For a few hours, I had the cell to myself and I thoroughly enjoyed it. It was stressing enough being in jail but I was hoping to get a cell by myself. Then entered my *"cellie"* who was an older white guy with a scruffy beard and a passion for jeopardy and poker. I thank God for his presence because he showed me how to adjust to jail culture. For starters, he advised me that if you don't eat the food, you will be hungry.

I learned how to manipulate my taste buds and my mind to eat whatever was on the tray. I learned the value of salt, pepper, peanut butter, and jelly. One of the odd moments occurred when I was wondering how to wash my boxers and socks because, at this point, I had them on for consecutive days. This was extremely uncomfortable for me. The shower water was ice cold and I wasn't sure if the soap even cleansed me. My skin was dry as a desert because I didn't have access to lotion. The towel that you bath with could barely fit a newborn baby. The conditions are designed to make you or break you and I refused to break. The life-changing moment occurred after I got out of the shower one night, climbed onto my bed and looked out the window the size of a cereal box opening. At this point, I was experiencing every emotion possible. I can't recall my exact words but they must have an effect on my cell buddy who said, *"Do you believe in God?"* And I responded with a loud and proud, *YES!* I saw a long hand extended toward the top bunk and it was his hand with a bible. It was a miniature copy of The Old Testament, The King James Version. I was still under the impression that I will be leaving jail soon, so I decided not to read it.

The next day—I received a glimmer of hope when my public defender made an appearance on the unit seeing another inmate. I went into a full-fledged sprint to get to him with the hope of hearing some good news. Right after I was taken into custody—I remember my public defender mentioning an appeal that could potentially get me out immediately. During our conversation—he gave me all of the information that I wanted to hear. This feel-good moment was only a superficial high because I never saw the public defender again. Go Figure! The next second, minutes, hours and days were a mentally awful and taxing place to be.

Walking around the unit, which was the size of a small family living room. Just imagine 50-60 guys cramped in this area with no access to leave. At different stages, the tension got so high because the *"wanna-be-gangstas"* attempted to impose their will on the phone and the TV. It made no sense to me because it only heightened the chances for a brawl to occur. The potential of a brawl caused me to never allow anyone to walk behind me without my first being balled up just in case things *"popped off."* The highlight of each day was receiving the sports section of the newspaper after it has been passed around the unit 10-15 times. It served as some semblance as to what was going on outside of jail. In addition to that, the occasional trivia battles stemming from the jeopardy episodes on TV. Occasionally, I would find myself laughing at some of the answers that the other inmates gave. I was fortunate enough to leave the unit for a few minutes and walk to the case manager's office. The case manager wasn't a pleasant person. His attitude had a shorter fuse than his physical appearance—almost to the point of being rude. The man apparently didn't have one caring bone in his petite body. The trip was helpful because it allowed me to inquire about working in the jail. One of the things that I heard from the multiple jail lawyers (other inmates) is that working makes the time go faster. I asked the case manager about working and he leaned over to the case manager in the adjacent cubicle and said, this guy wants to work. He said, I would be placed in the kitchen detail but he wasn't sure of how long the process would take. At this point, I was well accustomed to hurrying up and waiting. It's a natural process in jail.

I walked back to my cell and climbed onto my bed and attempted to prepare myself for a nap. Unfortunately for me- my anxiety was so high that I couldn't sleep. I guess it was a good thing because after tossing and turning, I got up and jumped off of the bunk bed. I instantly saw the old testament laying on the table. I immediately turned to the front of the bible and searched for scriptures on faith, understanding, patience, and perseverance. The feeling of reading the bible in jail was drastically different from my prior life before being detained. I have been in some valleys before but it was nothing like this. Battling alcoholism, being shot at close range, fighting depression and trying to discover myself were valleys that I eventually found my way to the peaks that were on the other side. It was almost as if the words were jumping off of the pages to me. The word of God was living and breathing like never before. Spending time with God becomes something that I desperately looked forward to and it provided a sense of peace in a chaotic world. I used to look forward to the *"count,"* which was the daily count of inmates throughout the jail because it forces inmates to be locked in. I used this as another opportunity to spend time with God and his word. I actually based on my reading schedule around lock-in times. Interestingly enough—the more I got locked in—the more freedom I experienced. Not only did I begin the process of working on my mental and spiritual strength, but I also started the process of transforming physically.

I noticed one inmate had a regular routine of pushups and sit-ups but I wasn't interested in befriending anyone. Eventually, we started to converse and found out we had similar interest like bettering the community by helping young people. I don't even think I remember his name, but I remembered he mentioned his struggles with alcohol. This was the perfect opportunity to share how God help me fight the spirit that held me in bondage for years. There was another over the top personality that kept gravitating towards me. I was amazed at his level of concern and care for the other inmates, particularly making sure that everyone had an opportunity to use the phone. In jail and prison, telephone time and good food is the closest thing to freedom that one could imagine. I was always skeptical of people's motives and this was certainly the case with this inmate. With each passing day—he continued to be the voice of reason and wanted everyone to be able to use the phone.

One instance stood out more than others-two older inmates who appeared to be in the mid-'70s walked on the unit and appeared to clueless about everything, including the protocol about using the phone. This inmate, called Skills, assisted the inmates in contacting family members and legal counsel. As I marched toward the phone one day, I didn't have a clue to use it because it required a pin number. Fortunately for me, Skills was right there and willing to assist me. Throughout my stay in the receiving area, we talked about each other charges and he reminded me, even though I didn't want to hear it, God allowed me to be in jail for my personal development and betterment. Skills was a jail veteran and continued to educate me about the process. He was willing to make trades with meals. I could always go to him and trade my fruit for extra bread, which was essential for peanut butter and jelly sandwiches. I got used to seeing familiar faces on the unit but there was one face that I was used to seeing in another detention center.

During my tenure at the Baltimore City Juvenile Justice Center— there were only a few young men who I approached with extreme caution. I vividly remember this young man spitting on and punching a staff member. His reputation was nothing short of a street legend, including a few bodies (murders). I walked out of my cell and saw this young man but he apparently didn't remember me. It was another taste of the humble pie and a refresher of how low I had sunk. He was detained on a handgun charge and ultimately given bail, but my trigger phone fingers were still sitting. Just as I was slowly but surely accumulating myself to the jail culture, including washing my boxers and socks in the sink every day and letting them dry overnight in my cell, and even putting them back on while they were partially wet—change had finally come.

Each day the CO's correctional officers would scream out 5-10 names and say "*Pack up.*" This packing up as wasn't an indication that you were going home as a free man, but rather you were going to another unit. My friend Skills advised me because my charges were non-violent in nature that I should be going to the new side. The new side had the best amenities that jail could offer. Two TV's on each unit, more tables and seating, and a better environment. It was kind of laughable what I started to appreciate. The old side lacked all of the aforementioned and it was a harsher environment. Finally, after a week, I got to explore another part of the jail. *Mills, pack up!* Even though, it was about 10:30 at night and I was sleepy, I was more than ready to go. It didn't take long to pack up my limited belongings and dump them in a net bag and sit by the door. After waiting for an hour- the next journey in my jail stay was about to happen.

The Blue Jumper

"As Iron sharpens Iron, so a man sharpens the countenance of his friend. **Proverbs 27:17 (CSB)**

The jail system often classifies inmates by the nature of their charges, which translates to the color of the jumper that you wear. After being told to walk in a single file to the right side of the hallway—I walked an area to picked up my new fashion statement which was the blue jumper. When I walked onto the unit, I was already familiar with the weird looks from the inmates. The CO on the unit had a rough exterior. He was short, bald, built like a hummer and he was dressed unlike the other CO's. He was in black cargo pants, black shirt, and black high-top boots. His outfit reminded me of the tactical squad members of the lockup shows that I used to be fascinated with. My suspicion was certainly correct. I would later find out that he was a part of the goon squad. The goon squad was a specific unit designed to respond before or after an incident of violence occurred. Normally their presence meant that someone was going to get roughed up and transported to the hole. From the stories that I heard and thank God it wasn't from personal experience—the hole a is two-person cell designed to break your very soul and dignity. You are only allowed out of your cell for one solitary hour and you don't have access to sunlight or phone calls.

This CO was barking orders at the new arrivals to stand in a corner while he and the other officers continued to shakedown the unit. The shakedown was a process to ensure that drugs, weapons, and any other forms of contraband were not in the unit. All of the inmates were watching as the officers went from cell to cell. Each unit had four cells doors on the bottom and four at the top. Within each cell door, the capacity existed to house 6 inmates. There were two sets of bunk beds and two individual beds. The inmates were peeking out of their door rooms like kids looking out the window waiting for momma and daddy to return home. The shakedown lasted longer than I had anticipated, but I was gradually getting better with the fact that I wasn't the "*man*" that I thought I was and nobody moved on my time. This was an extremely difficult concept for me to master. God was slowly, but surely grooming me in this area.

Eventually, I settled into my new dorm and sleeping area. I was still pissed off about the whole idea of being detained so I was ready to pop off and blow up at anybody. My bunk buddies annoyed the hell out of me with their politeness as I walked in the room. Two of them stood out more than others for different reasons. I was immediately struck by the braids that she wore. Yes, *her* braids!! Her name was Shakira. She was a woman who was making the transition from an African-American male to a female. Despite her young age, apparently nineteen to about twenty-two, she was a jail regular and knew all of the loopholes. She had all of the CO's down to a science. She knew what CO's who were more lenient than others. She and another inmate had a love/hate relationship that consisted of them talking/ joking/ and arguing with each other every night. It was the equivalent of two juveniles in grade school fighting with each other because they liked each other. It felt like they were on the cast of *Seinfeld* or some other sitcom. I must admit that their goofiness begins to become a peace that I needed and welcomed. I was literally laughing myself to sleep at night.

One of the main guys who keep me in tears was a big dude by the name of Austin, probably 6'2 and built like an NFL player. He had a fiery red goatee but his sense of humor and sarcasm reminded me of my own. After our nightly lock in—I peeked over and saw him engaged in reading, which is one of my passions. While I continued to read my bible, he was reading a bigger, different version of the bible. This version is written specifically for inmates. I eventually broke down and asked him if he had any reading material. I already knew he did but it was my own way of breaking the ice. He kindly obliged and I suddenly found myself with a new friend and new reading material.

Throughout the boredom that each day on the unit brings—I found myself engrossed in the word of God, especially with access to multiple bibles. I was comparing the language and meaning that I received from different versions. As a lifelong learner and reader, I welcomed this unexpected study time. It's interesting how God places people together from different backgrounds, experiences, skills, etc. for one common goal which is to bring him glory and honor. Looking at this from a traditional lens, Austin and I were not supposed to be friends because I thought we didn't have anything in common. For instance, Austin was educated by his mom via homeschooling, then he was able to attend one of Baltimore's premier private school on a lacrosse scholarship. This was a far cry from my educational upbringing in public schools.

Austin didn't have the demeanor of someone who was a jailhouse regular. I observed an individual that wanted to learn from his mistake and quickly be reunited with his family. Interestingly enough, this was his first major experience with people of color, especially men of color.

Unfortunately, I looked around the unit and saw predominantly black men. It was really disheartening for me because I allowed myself to slip into the statistic of black men and incarceration. Austin and I would discuss our upbringings and his father passed at an early age and he was forced to be the man of the house. I understand his situation completely because my biological father has been incarcerated on/off for nearly thirty years. We both expressed our love for fatherhood with our children and the joys associated with it. Austin would often tell me about some of his hobbies like hunting and I kindly said I would pass on any invitation. We both got a good laugh out of that.

One of the things that I admired about Austin was his computer like memory as it relates to the word of God. I would begin to ask him every day about chapters, verses, meaning, history and etc. I had the good fortune of attending the divinity school known as the Baltimore County Detention Center. For some reason, my commissary hadn't quite arrived yet—so I was trying to survive off of the food and that wasn't going so well. I would hear groans at night and it was coming from the area of my body known as my stomach. One of the lessons that I was being taught is to put your pride aside and ask for help. Austin had a locker full of good snacks and I asked for some help and he was more than willing to assist me. This unit had some shady looking characters and for some reason—I felt a fight will soon happen. I was almost sure that the fight wouldn't involve me because I made it my business to stay clear of any trouble. One day in the day area which consisted of limited seating and is normally filled with the typical noise of card playing, (which I don't know how to play), I saw a few guys sitting across from each other at the table. Both were rumored to be a part of a jail gang. They were conversing, which quickly grew to argue, and then suddenly both parties stood up. No one paid them any attention because guys argue all the time. After all, this is jail. Frustrations and tensions are at an all-time high. I assumed that the disagreement was a result of a card game. Before I knew it, I heard a loud screeching sound which was the hard rubber chair being slid across the room.

LET'S GET READY TO RUMBLE!! Both parties stepped from the table and before I could blink, a third party moved in the picture. A few punches were thrown and one of them landed and I heard a loud thunderous sound. The sound was followed by an object flying in the air. That object was a tooth flying from one of the inmates' mouth. At this time, the CO has called for the goon squad to come to clean up the mess. Surprisingly, all of the inmates involved calmed down and voluntarily placed their hands behind their backs. When the goon squad arrived, they politely cuffed and took the inmates to lock up. This was not like the scene of a jailhouse fight that is typically shown on TV. When it was over, the conversation focused on what was the cause of it. I found out that it was due to a debt owed, but the truly surprising part to learn was the debt was a pack of ramen noodles. What!! Additionally, I learned that the participants were in the same gang. So much for loyalty, I guess. In the only fight, I witnessed in my three months stay—this incident reinforced the importance of the principality, no matter how big or small. My stay in the unit wasn't that much longer. In the next 72 hours, I heard the sweet sound of *"Mills, pack up."*

The Green Jumper

For the Scripture says, *"Do not muzzle an ox while it treads out the grain,"* and *"The worker deserves his wages."* **I Timothy 5:18 (NIV)**

I was familiar with the process of packing up, receiving a new wardrobe and moving on. For an individual who has hated changed; I greatly welcomed it. I was ecstatic because I knew this move was attached to gaining employment. Prior to my detainment, I had a few jobs and earned a decent living. After receiving the forest green jumper, which was oversized. The best tailor in the world couldn't make the adjustments to properly fit me. Despite the fact, I was still mad, frustrated, and still, in partial disbelief, I was adjusting to the culture more and more.

When I walked onto this unit, I knew I wouldn't see any fights or experience a high level of confusion because everyone was working, which reduced the tension. While standing in the front of unit, I heard a familiar voice scream, *"What's up, Mr. Bowtie Mills?"* Before I could decipher whose voice, it was—I saw the familiar face attached to the voice. He ran over and give me a handshake, followed by a big hug. He never appeared to be in shock that we were now in the same predicament. Just a few months ago, he was a detainee at the juvenile justice center and I was providing him with therapeutic services. It's funny how quickly things change, and sometimes it's not always for the better. He was a big guy with a huge smile, extremely gregarious with an incredible ability to dance like Michael Jackson and a good sense of humor to boot. His was previously detained for a horrific charge and I was able to give him insight on the poor choices that he made. He was always receptive to the information. As a result of him being detained for so long, I was able to develop a relationship with him. I felt like he was a son to me and now we were in the same place. I initiated that the fact I had done something less than wise and I was sorry. I was prepared for him to say, "*How could you tell us to the right thing and you aren't doing it?*" He was the total opposite. "*Mr. Mills, if you need anything-I got you.*" He was ready to fight for me if I needed some assistance. I would eventually get him to give me some noodles and Doritos before my first commissary order arrived. Life is really a full circle of people and places. It always comes back around.

After I found my cell assignment—I walked in and climbed up on the top bunk and sat on the dusty, dirty green mattress that probably had bed bugs on it and reflected. The self-reflection was all of the choices that I made and the people were impacted. My mind started telling me that I was a fraud and I couldn't use my own advice and use the therapeutic skills on myself. The same skills that I had helped countless people, especially young men of color in the past. My mind was telling me that my beautiful kids would hate me because I neglected to consider my responsibility to them by making a bad choice.

After a nap, I woke up and met one of my new cell buddies. He was a big guy with more tattoos than me. He was extremely polite but I noticed that he had a slight drawl in his speech. Later that same evening, I noticed the pace in which he walked was extremely slow and everything about him seem to be delayed. The therapist in me noticed everything and begin to do a mental case study. It was roughly about 8pm and he was preparing for bed voluntarily. This behavior was odd, considering that most inmates hate to lock in and wanted to push the boundaries of staying up late. Right before he laid down, a few inmates came in the room and they begin whispering. Then one of them started discussing numbers and prices, and he pulled out a balled-up napkin. He opened the napkin and used his pinky finger to put a clear strip on the table. It was my first introduction to the rampant drug world in jail.

They agreed on a price and the date of the payment. My cell buddy popped it in his mouth and proceeded to sleep a short time later. I never asked questions because it wasn't my concern at all. Before the night had concluded, I meet all of my new bunk buddies and they all seemed to be cool. One of them stated, *"Mills, I heard from someone else that you worked at the juvenile jail in the city,"* and I responded that I did. He warned me that I would probably know many of his friends who were previously detained there. After a few minutes of conversation, he was absolutely right. His co-defendants on the charges that he was currently detained for were youth that I had worked within days before my detainment.

More self-reflection occurred and I begin to mentally beat myself up. The following day he called home and spoke with one of them who had been recently released. This particular youth's response to my detainment was a nightmare for me. He was critical of me being detained and stated that I was not better than anyone else. I guess, to a degree he was right. Since I arrived in this unit with employment already in place. I knew it was only a matter of time before I start working.

Everyone had on the unit had a job working inside the jail. The jobs included the jail kitchen, laundry detail, and the floor detail. Luckily for me, I had already been selected to work the kitchen detail. After two days, I was ready to start working. My name has never been synonymous with hard laborious work; however, I was ready to start working. My eagerness wasn't hampered by the salary of $1 a day. More than half of the unit worked in the day and the other half worked at night.

On my first official work day—I had no idea what to expect. My buddies told me that one of the benefits of working in the jail kitchen was access to bigger portions of food. Even though the food was disgusting- I figured I could get full from it. When we got to the kitchen area- it brought back memories of the jobs that I had at 15 and 16 years of age working in the fast food industry. It was a big kitchen filled with the largest oven and stove that I had ever seen. I briefly walked around and I was instantly reminded that this is jail! Near one of the cutting stations- I noticed two large knives that were bolted down, assuring that the user could only use for them cutting food and not someone's throat.

After about 30 minutes of standing around- my lack of patience was starting to kick in. After all, I still believed that my name held some kind of importance. I was still stuck in the mentality that I wasn't supposed to be in my jail and this was a mistake and people should move swiftly to accommodate me. *THAT DIDN'T HAPPEN*! Finally, I heard a loud, rough voice bark out instructions that startled me. She reminded me of a grandmother who administered tough love. She was short and based on her walk, she had been in the service industry and standing on her feet a long time. Her rapport with the inmates solidified that she cared for and respected them, but she was also in the business of getting her job done. I introduced myself and she quickly said, "*I will be with you shortly.*" Eventually, she got back with me said, "*look on the list and see what is next to your name.*" I scrolled down the list and saw Coleslaw next to my name and I immediately thought that I didn't even eat coleslaw. And before I could go to her and ask another question, she just pointed in the direction of the serving line, which would be my home for the next 10.5 hours a day, and the next 7-10 days. I was briefed on what to do, which wasn't overly complicated.

I was given 5 or 6 huge tubs of coleslaw and one gigantic spoon and told not to put too much on each tray. I replied by asking the question, "how many trays do we need to put them on"? Maybe I should've asked that question because the answer was overwhelming when I heard it. Every tray for every inmate in the building. Wait, that shouldn't be too bad because from the looks of the jail on the outside-it wasn't big enough to house too many inmates. I would find the hard way that it houses over 1000 inmates. Guess who was responsible for placing a scoop of runny, disgusting coleslaw on each of the ugly, brown, thick trays? *ME!* Within the first ten minutes, I wanted to quit but what was the alternative. Also, it was rumored that if you quit, you lose the job, go to lock up and go the old side of the jail.

None of those choices seemed to be pleasing to me. As the trash was thrown down the line, I tried to find creative minds games that would make it easier. At one point, I was reciting bible verses in my mind, rapping and singing, and thinking about my babies. Not one of them worked and made time go by any faster. However—I found myself repeating the lyrics to the theme song of the sitcom called *Good Times*. *Good Times* was a sitcom from the 1970s about an African-American family's' daily struggles of living in the ghetto. I was singing *Keeping your head above water, Makin' a wave when you can. Temporary Layoffs, Good times*! Hanging in the chow line, Good times. Upon my release—I delivered a sermon called *God Times*, detailing how God elevated me during my jail stay.

At this point—my feet and ears were killing me equally. My feet were hurting from all of the standing in one place, and my ears were hurting from all of the glorified gangsta stories. Apparently, everyone was living the life of the fictional character *Scarface* in the community. When I realized that we finished the lunch rush, I rewarded myself by making countless peanut butter and jelly sandwiches and sitting down in a makeshift break room. I sat on a crate and realized how thirsty I was and I noticed the syrup like juice in a bag. It was called base and it doubled as a floor stain. Yes—the same juice in bags was used on the same floors. I briefly thought about it and realized how thirsty I was and decided to drink one or two. My belly was full and the thirst had been quenched and before I knew it, I was fast asleep.

After resting my laurels—I quickly jumped up from nap land—hearing that same loud voice hollering out, *"It's time for water world."* I thought to myself, what is the *water world*? It sounded like an amusement park but there was nothing amusing about anybody's jail. *Water World* was the section at the back of the kitchen that held all of the equipment to wash the dishes. My mother could attest that washing dishes wasn't a good skill set that I had, so I made it up in my mind to put my best foot forward.

The process involved dumping the trash off of the trays, running them through a washing machine, and then through a huge dryer. After the lunch duties were completed, it was time to repeat the same process for dinner. For me—It was scooping out coleslaw or some other less than edible side and washing dishes. Toward the end of my first day, I looked down at my green jumper and noticed it was black. It was filled with food particles, water stains and trash. I was actually proud of myself that I had actually earned full days wage of one dollar. When I arrived back on the unit, I didn't have the energy to talk with anyone because I was exhausted.

Every day I was discovering new revelations from within me and learning lessons from God about my own constitution. I had discovered a new sense of humility and appreciation for hard work. The feeling of being doused with more gratitude than ever before overwhelmed my spirit. All of the aforementioned qualities were already present *in me*— but apparently—God needed for me to get reacquainted with them again. My attentions were absolutely undivided as my focus had to be sharp on the inside. As I became more familiar with the process in the kitchen—I was able to manage it much more effectively. Many of the younger inmates called me *old head*, as we would argue about basketball and music with me providing *the correct* perspective from an old school point of view. During the breaks between the shifts, I would pull out the bible and begin to read the Word. One day, I noticed that the other inmates were doing the same. I was thrilled to see it and even more thrilled that we started to have discussions about God and his Holy Word. It was dawning on me that multiple times over the week I noticed the other inmates actively reading and discussing the daily bread devotionals. There were many moments like this where the presence of God could be seen and felt. I begin looking forward to reading and discussing the word of God with other inmates.

Eventually, I got my first check which equaled $5 and I was happy to get it because I know the type of effort that went into it earning it. It was at that this juncture that I would make a mental note of this feeling; in a new place of discernment, I could see that moving forward, I will dedicate myself to remaining humble and never allow money to define me as a person. A new understanding brought me to a realization that at any given time—you can lose everything that you have ever worked for and be reduced down to unimagined lows. In the next week, I settled into a routine and adjusted accordingly to live in the kitchen. I would joke with myself and say *I moved up from serving coleslaw to serving cake and cornbread!*

In the midst of being in hell—I continued to appreciate the little things. Sometimes I was required to take the trash into the hallways and I would see other inmates outside working on the dock. My curiosity immediately began to heighten and I wondered, how can I get to where they are. I was advised by a friend to contact on unit leadership to put in a request to switch jobs. He informed me that the success rate isn't that high because the jail views working as a privilege and they don't take kindly to the idea of changing jobs. This was a reminder that God has the final say in all matters. The inmates were working on the dock, which was the area that received the food and supplies needed to feed the inmates. Since the pay for both jobs was the same, I needed to really to determine was it worth it. Some of the deciding factors were the attire (wearing your own clothes) and access to better food. I noticed the inmates on the dock were in civilian clothes. One of the older inmates that I had befriended came in the break room between shifts and said, *"Mills, do you want some chicken fingers and fries?"* and of course I replied with a loud, *"of course!"* I initially thought he was playing a mean-spirited trick on me until I saw the Styrofoam container and smelled the familiar aromas. It was a small slice of heaven on earth (*The Little Things*).

Before my detainment—I enjoyed the freedoms of eating what I wanted and when I wanted to eat—so I normally would not have been this excited. I had one chicken finger and a handful of fries and it was so refreshing to my mind. I thought I had tasted freedom but after hearing *"It's time for a water world,"* I quickly reminded myself that I was *still inmate #458627*. I wanted to experience God's natural air. One of the things that I took for granted was the beauty of nature. Simply things like hearing and watching the raindrops fall, hearing a bird's morning song, feeling the heat from the rays of God's sunshine on top of me. Being in jail takes away nature because you are so isolated from it, other than the occasional glimpse outside of the short window. The air is stale and extremely cold and I think it's done intentionally to further break down a man's spirit. I would continue to place a request to the leadership department that handles the jobs in the jail. Of course, I didn't get a response for days at a time. Once again—I found myself laughing because I knew God was using this as another opportunity to mold me into the person that he needed me to be. I knew that my struggle with patience was being tested in jail—waiting on someone else to move was the ultimate lesson learned.

At this point, I continued to work and wait. I had grown accustomed to jail. When I placed my first commissary order (junk food and hygiene supply from the jail store), the jail wasn't so bad after all. I never thought my mind would conceive of such a thought. One of the unexpected highlights of being detained was watching the ingenious nature of my fellow inmates. If you are not familiar with jail culture— you may not understand the term, "*hookup*." The *hookup* is the finest form of jail cuisine. It requires noodles (ramen noodles) and many packets of them. The noodles are cooked in the microwave and then spread out on a plastic bag. Depending on your taste buds—you can add cheese, sausage, pickles, tuna, packaged chicken and then level it all up with the seasoning packet. All of the ingredients are then added into a bowl and you have the best that jail can offer. Without thinking about it—I had morphed into the jail culture—but two major elements were still missing from my life.

Daddy's Girls

"Behold, children are a heritage from the Lord" **Psalms 127:3 (NKJV)**

God has blessed me in immeasurable ways throughout the course of my life. Two of his mighty blessings stand out more than any others. He allowed me to become a father of two beautiful twin girls. God's grace was on display throughout the pregnancy and subsequent birth. Cynthia experienced some complications that required her to be on bed rest for an extended period of time. I wasn't aware that having twins is high risk due to a variety of reasons. For my girls, one was taking more nutrients from her sibling. As a result—Cynthia had to see a world-renowned specialist who had experience working with twins. Every day for several weeks at a time, she had to go to the hospital to make sure that the smaller of the two didn't die in her womb. It was an incredibly frightening experience. I was well aware that the girls would be born premature and I was ready, or so I thought, for fatherhood. I was thrilled with the idea of being a father, even though I have never witnessed fatherhood from any firsthand experience. My biological father has been incarcerated for the majority of my life. However; my grandfather was an awesome role model—but I didn't see or interact with him on a daily basis, even though we spent a lot of time together.

On June 2, 2009, while working as a teacher assistant, I remember vividly hearing my name being yelled on the intercom. I ran to the main office like someone was chasing me and I picked up the phone. It was their aunt and she said. *"Rashad, they are taking the babies and you need to get to the hospital.*" I sprinted across the parking lot, jumped in my car, and got to the hospital in what felt like seconds. After finding my way to their mom and sister in the hospital room, my nervousness took over and I paced back and forth over a hundred plus times. In addition to this—I couldn't stop using the restroom and I think I drank about two or three sodas. Finally, it was showtime. I put on the hospital gown, headwear and followed their mom in tow with the team of doctors and nurses into the delivery room. The doctors were so skillful at delivering babies that they were talking about horse racing and who to bet on for future races. I'm on pins and needles and they were laughing and joking.

At 4:40pm, I heard a cry that would alter the coursing of my life. She was tiny but beautiful. And before I knew it, at 4:41, another beautiful, even tinier baby had arrived. Seeing them before my eyes was a feeling that I had never experienced before. I was in awe because I witnessed two miracles right in front of me. They were 3lbs, 12 oz, and 2lbs, 1oz respectively. From that day going forward—I have and will forever be in love with my kids. Since their birth, I have been blessed enough to see them almost every day. I couldn't recall a period that my babies were too far out of my reach until now that I was *inmate 458627,* taking an unexpected vacation. There were days that I tried to do what I advised my clients not to do, which is to suppress emotions. I tried to forget about the idea that I was not able to see my kids or talk with them on a regular basis. The pain was indescribable and like nothing, I have experienced before. It was pure torment. Will asked me what was I going to tell my kids and I was puzzled, to say the least. I have never had to deal with a situation similar to this from the perspective of a parent, but I have had too much experience from the perspective of a child with a parent in jail or prison. I made the mistake of not consulting God first for direction and guidance and it turned out to be a bad decision. The story or lie had quickly turned into me working in New York. The shame and guilt that I carried with me each day were awful. Sometimes my bunk bed would feel like my coffin. I felt dead to the world due to a lack of connection with my kids.

There were times that I didn't want to talk to them on the phone because they were bombarding me with questions and I didn't want the lie to grow bigger and bigger. I sensed the same regret and unspeakable pain that my biological father must have felt communicating with me when I was younger. By the age of 13, I had already been in federal prisons in different states visiting him. My father, whom I loved dearly and considered to be one of the smartest people I know, has given jails, and the prison systems across the country the majority of his life. My brother and I learned to communicate with him via phone calls and letters.

The generational curse of incarceration has been a recurring theme for my family. I can recall three of my family members who collectively have been sentenced to over 100 years and served over 60 years. I desperately wanted to avoid being another man in my bloodline allowing his mistakes to lead to jail and prison and kill the connection with his family due to his absence. More importantly, kill the dreams for himself. Due to my father's nonexistence growing up—my brother has since decided to sever all ties with him. I have and will continue to pray for the Day of Reconciliation between the two. I was determined to break this wretched cycle, even with my mistakes.

The missing element of a man's presence often times left me trying to figure manhood on my own. My feelings of discontentment turned into love and understanding when I got into the streets. It was easier for me to connect with him because I knew how easy you can get into trouble and how hard it is to get out. Oddly enough—during my detainment—we were still communicating via jail mail. *Inmate 458627* would write to *228319*. I couldn't locate the emotions inside of me that would describe the feeling of being an incarcerated father, writing to another incarcerated father. Ironically, I was worried that he would be disappointed in me, but it was quite the opposite. He still showed love and support. This is a part of me that believes he was concerned I was throwing away my life. I was hoping my girls wouldn't be disappointed in me.

The internal battle that I was dealing with was a level of hell on Earth I wished on no man, and jail is not exactly the place to deal with mental health issues. Truthfully, I would imagine jail exacerbates all mental health issues, but luckily God kept me sane. The clinician in me saw people suffering from obvious signs of depression and anxiety, but I didn't see any help readily available for the needs of these men. It gnawed at my spirit; the circumstance was really sad to witness. Although, I never saw them personally—I was informed that mental health assistance was available. A glimmer of hope...

I was deliberate and intentional not to call the kids no more than once a week. With each call I would go over the daily affirmation that we would recite in the morning and at night: *God loves you; I love you, you're beautiful, smart, and you can have anything in the world if you work hard for it.* Two days after my release—I would own up to the most difficult task of telling them of the mistakes that I made. For an individual who loves to talk—I struggled to find the words. In addition to finding words or sentences that accurately represented anything resembling an explanation of my absence. We had just finished having dinner together and preparing to have a snack. I thought it was time for the truth. Luckily, my kids haven't been exposed to much and I don't believe they understand the concept of jail. Quite frankly, I'm glad they don't. I had practiced the scenario in my mind on several occasions, but practice doesn't make perfect in this instance.

My voice was cracking and I stuttered on several times but I managed to get out the following: *"daddy made some stupid mistakes and cross several boundaries and went to jail."* After I finished—one of the twins who was literally playing with her feet said, *"Okay, can we go play checkers now?"* I expressed the hardest thing ever and her competitive nature took over and she wanted to play me in a board game! I wanted to laugh but I looked in the direction of her sister and it wasn't a laughing matter. The oldest of the two had a tear on the cusp of coming out and I was screaming inside, *"please don't cry!!"* I knew if she cried—I was going to be flowing like a river. She said, *"Daddy, I don't even want my snack and I'm ready to go to sleep."* As I walked behind her up the steps—I couldn't stand myself for the pain I caused.

Since this conversation—my time away has never resurfaced again but I believe as they get older, more questions would need to be answered. From this day forward, I have vowed to never be in any predicament that jeopardizes my presence with my kids.

My Friends

"A Man who has friends must himself be friendly. But there is a friend who sticks closer than a brother." **Proverbs 18:24 (NKJV)**

Many of the opportunities that were offered to me while detained were as a result of the powerful support system that I had on the outside. Due to the unexpected nature of my detainment—I was totally blind-sided—and couldn't have been prepared to handle my affairs. From day one, Will played the role of friend, brother, financial adviser, mentor, liaison, public relations director and any other name for that matter. Within seconds of learning my fate from the judge—I called him and told him the not-so good news. His initial response was *"are you kidding?"* and of course, I wasn't. Will sprang into action and made his way to the courthouse and picked up some of my belongings like car keys and telephone. I called him so many times in the first 48 hours that he was probably sick of me. He literally had a checklist of responsibilities that I needed to handle, in the order from most to least important.

Will's level of calm was so welcoming for me because I was a complete train wreck inside. One of the tasks that he did was reaching out to everyone in my phone and let them know what had occurred. Prior to my detainment—I had a lot of activities scheduled like teaching public speaking and a variety of speaking engagements scheduled. He stepped up and called, texted, and communicated on my behalf. One of the things that he had to do was try to provide a sense of calm to my mother. My mother was supportive, loving, and caring. I think she felt more pain than I did. That was a gigantic sized task because she was caught off guard by everything. Will made sure that I had money to make the phone call and he answered every one of my calls, no matter the hour. I don't think I could've asked for any more, but he provided it. One of the reasons that I was able to have so much and quickly moved from one job to another was his relationship with one of the work release/job coordinators. My daughters made it to summer camp every day and all of their swimming lessons because of him. It was so important to note that he did all of this while being a husband, father, and a businessman. I'm forever indebted and grateful to him for this. He was my literal *Superman*!

I have always believed that true friendship requires a certain level of sacrifice. In addition to this, true friends may not talk for a while but when one is in need—the other is there without asking any questions. Chuck has been, and still remains, my GUY! Chuck and I ran the streets of Baltimore doing all of the partying, drinking and dancing that one could imagine. We were legends for being the first and last on the dance floor. We never met a party or drink that we didn't like. When I decided to change my life—we went different ways and I thought it took some time for us to understand that we were still brothers, just on different paths. When he heard of my situation he immediately went into action and bought clothes, socks and other much-needed items. Without them—the experience would have been so much harder to cope with. All of my friends stated the following: *mistakes happen, but it's the recovery that determines how this story ends.*

The Dump

"He brought me up out of the pit of destruction, out of the miry clay, and he set my feet upon a rock making my footsteps firm." **Psalm 40:2 (KJV)**

Mills, pack your clothes because you are moving. I was familiar with this process by now. To be honest, I was happy because with each move—I was getting closer to an outside job and more freedom and with each day—I was getting closer to my ultimate goal of being released. My green jumper was traded in for a faded grey jumper. When I walked onto the work release unit, I saw my friend Austin and luckily for me, he was one of my bunkmates again. These circumstances let me know I was surrounded by at least one individual that I trusted, and more importantly—I would be able to discuss my Lord and Savior, Jesus Christ freely. Austin and I continued to build a deeper friendship and eventually, he would see of all the flawed parts of me. God will use people to make you aware of the parts of you that need to be fixed. After multiple nights where I battled verbally with correctional officers about the rules that I hated. Austin pulled me aside and said, *"you are a God-fearing hothead." What??* He continued by saying, *"I know you love God but you are a hot head and need to calm down."* For every moment thereafter in which my alter ego and arrogance surfaced—I reminded myself that I had to room to work on me.

One of the new amenities that I saw immediately was the basketball court on the unit. This was a major upgrade from the previous unit.

I was happy to see only three of us shared this space. Austin, Neil, Hayden and I were sharing the uncomfortable space. For a few days—I wanted to get a response from the work release department about my start date. Sitting on the unit while everyone went to work was maddening. I actually started watching daytime television to kill time. Sleeping the boredom away was not an option for me despite being all up night. My cell was positioned near the main door, which was an entrance to the unit. I heard all of the morning traffic from the other inmates going to work at 3am, and the nurse yelling *MEDICATION* at 3:45, and the *FEED UP* call at 4am. Opportunity knocked when I finally met with the work release department and I was granted permission to work on the dock. I didn't have access to my outside clothing yet and of the guards directed me to a closest and provided me some with hand me downs.

The pants were two waists too big and the shoes were a whole size too big. *Alright, Rashad, you have worked a job for one dollar per day and not per hour. Surely the pay of $20 at the dump was worthy of any labor you had to endure. This should be pretty easy!* This is what I was telling myself when I was awakened up at 5am by the correctional officer's voice through the intercom system. Just as I was trying to trick myself and funnel positive thoughts in my head—I realized that I was still upset because I was in jail, and about to work in a trash dump. I adhere to the saying, *"wearing my emotions on my sleeve,"* because everyone I encountered in hallways and boarding the bus looked at me and asked, *"Are you alright?"* And my response was *No!!!* Being on a bus and actually leaving the jail should have been exciting, but that was blocked by my anger. I looked at the other inmates as they talked and laughed and sang the country music songs that came on the radio. I wondered how they could be comfortable in this environment. During the short bus ride—I remember pondering the following thoughts; *how are my kids doing? Does God still care for me? And Lord—when is my release date?*

As we arrived, my eyes instantly gravitated to an opening in the building and I saw a huge mountain full of trash. After stepping off of the bus, I smelled an odor that my nose has never been smelled before. It was unbearable and I tried to hold my breath and that would have been impossible to do for a period of eight to ten hours a day. As we walked in the breakroom area, which was covered in dust and filth, and I kept saying to myself that this can't be real. I quickly signed in to ensure that I got paid and then I grabbed my hard hat and protective goggles and mask and walked upstairs to my work zone. The sound of the machines was so loud that I couldn't even process my angry thoughts. Each machine was receiving trash from another machine and then funneling it to another. The inmate's roles were to sort all of the trash in the designated trash areas. I was under the impression that trash was trash and it didn't need to be categorized. I waited for a few minutes before I was assigned to separate plastic bottles from aluminum.

I was fighting an incredible mental battle in my mind. My emotions and thoughts were swirling like a tornado and ranged from not doing any work at all—coupled with walking out of the dump and running for my freedom. *Yes*, I was so sick of being detained that I thought about being an escapee. There was a huge opening at the dump that would have served as an easy opportunity to walk out and experience temporary freedom. I couldn't believe that this was a realistic option that was in my mind. As I continued to halfheartedly toss bottles around—I decided that it wasn't worth it to extend my time by being an escapee.

I didn't know how much longer I could mentally manage in this environment. In the immediate moments—I needed to devise a plan that would allow the time to go by faster. My initial thought was to find a hiding spot in the building and sleep. So, I decided that I was going to explore the building and I was going to do it via my bathroom break.

I walked over to the makeshift office that had all of the correctional officers in it and I walked in. Before I could utter the words about needing to go to the bathroom: they leaped up and in a very aggressive tone, asked me if I could read. I replied by stating that I could and a lot better than either one of them. Apparently, I missed the sign on the door that stated, *PLEASE KNOCK BEFORE ENTERING.* It wasn't done intentionally but it led to a heated debate. One of them stated that they didn't like my attitude when I boarded the bus and they were adamant that working was a privilege and if I didn't like the rules, I could quit. Strangely enough—I was waiting for this opportunity to release more venom off of my chest and I fired back with a barrage of vulgarities and it felt good. I stormed out of the office and walked back to my station. I managed to settle into a groove and work to the best of my ability. During critical moments of my life, I often visualized better moments to help me get through. As I continued to sift through the trash, I started having images of me sharing this story on a stage encouraging others that you make it through the darkest times of your life. I was literally reciting things like one man's trash is another man's treasure. I had industrial earbuds in my ears to block the noise of the machine, but I was still able to hear the loud scream of other inmates, *"Yo, it's a rat!"* As quickly as I heard the sounds of the screams—I noticed all of the inmates running away from the conveyor belt. Before I could manage to move—I saw a dead rat the size of a football pass by. The rat was completely mangled from going through a variety of machines, designed to rip and shred. If the sight of it wasn't bad enough, the ghastly smell of it was so God awful that I nearly vomited. It was a dreadful experience and took me back to the idea that I should quit and risk life in lock up or just escape.

After getting a much-needed lunch break, I returned to the same spot only to hear a supervisor tell me that he has been watching me and I haven't been working to his standard. This was an added insult to the mental injuries that I had already endured. Another verbal altercation occurred and I had an anger/ frustration in me that I never know existed. As I stared outside—I felt emotionally overwhelmed and I was feeling out of sorts. The abnormal feeling was the result of a tear that slowly trickled down my face. I promised myself that I wouldn't cry during this experience. My counseling experience told me that it is healthy and therapeutic to engage in a good cry. I would have an internal dialogue with myself and laugh and say, *"Rashad, one tear doesn't constitute as crying."* After a few days—I absolutely hated everything about this job. Any brokenness that was in me was heightened by the job at the dump.

I apologized to the staff for my behavior because God continually re-minded me that it isn't their fault. The dump was designed to break me mentally and physically but I wouldn't allow it. Let me rephrase that and say—God *won't* allow me to be broken.

There were several moments that had me on the cusp of breaking. For example, as I boarded the bus after the long, grueling shift had ended, I sat down near the first set that I saw. My feet and legs were screaming due to the intense pain that we're going through them. If felt like sharp spikes every time I walked. I remember seeing an open seat and I quickly sat down. As I sat down and untied my shoes, I was obliv-ious to the inmate that was behind me in the line. As I looked up—I saw an angry face, accompanied by the words—*this is my assigned seat*. I quickly tied my shoes again because I felt he was a threat and I had enough frustration in my system that I was more than ready to re-lease. Once again—I didn't use any therapeutic skills to defuse the situation. I actually heightened it by expressing myself in the most un-pleasant manner possible. There weren't any assigned seats and my initial reaction was he was trying to get over on me. I stood up and we had a momentary stare down. Luckily, one of the older, more respected inmates told me that he wasn't attempting to disrespect me, but the seat had meaning to him. *What could've been the meaning behind a sweaty rubber seat on a hot, crowded, bus-back-to jail?* The inmate whispered to me that he and other inmates sit near each other and trade, smuggle drugs and other contraband that were stolen back into the jail. It made perfect sense and I was more than willing to apologize.

Later that night, a blessing came in the form of one of the correctional officers. She was short with a petite figure, serious mindset and was all business. Her style of communication with the inmates was a different correlation to her size. I believe that she wanted everyone to know that despite her size—*I will make sure that you respect me.* She was making her rounds during the shift change to complete the count and check ID bracelets. and I sitting up on my bunk. She immediately noticed the size of my leg and starting asking questions. She made a suggestion to put in a 118 and request to see the nurse and inform them I was unable to perform the required duties. I thanked her for the information but I skeptical because many people (not all) are looking for reasons to disqualify you from future employment. I figured with my gift to gab I was able to get out of working at the dump and still remain in good graces.

Nothing happens quickly or at a good time in jail. In the middle of the night—I heard my name screamed through the intercom system in the room to get up and get dressed and go to medical. Upon arriving in the medical department—I explained to the nurse the level of discomfort that I was dealing with. The nurse was an overly gregarious individual eager to help. She used her finger to examine my leg and she felt a rigid object in my leg. When I informed her that the object was a bullet fragment- she responded with a loud, Whoa!!! In 1997, I was in a period of trying to discover myself and found myself engaged in activities that were well over my head. For example, I was setting people up to be robbed, selling bad drugs to get money only to buy more drugs, in addition to selling counterfeit money. All of this was an attempt to fit in with the people I was hanging with. One night in one of the tougher neighborhoods in West Baltimore while selling heroin—two people had approached my buddies and I. When I knew what was happening—I grabbed my gun and froze momentarily as a result—I was shot at close range. By the grace of God—the bullet didn't shred my leg completely. It caused enough damage to have me in the hospital for nine days. The doctors performed a fasciotomy, which is a limb-saving procedure used to treat acute compartment syndrome. In essence- I could have lost my leg and suffered permanent nerve damage. Due to the severe nature and trauma of the injury, the doctors decided to leave the bullets fragments in. I was able to lead a normal life and compete in long distance running like marathons without any issues.

She immediately had x-rays ordered and explained that she would provide documentation so I wouldn't have to work at the dump. To say that I was elated would be an understatement at best. I would rather face the boredom of staying in the jail until another job surfaced then go back to the dump. Within a few days—I was called to the medical department again and the same nurse showed the x-rays and asked if I wanted the fragments removed. It was an interesting question for me because I always heard that it isn't a good idea to open an old wound because of the chance for it to get infected. There was a part of me that was excited to have them removed because they are very painful at times. I didn't contemplate long and decided to have them removed. Since I was still waiting to be assigned another job and didn't have to go to work, I didn't mind if the medical staff came and got me in the middle of the night for this procedure. And, of course, they did. I was under the impression that I would be transferred to a hospital for this procedure. The nurse informed me she had all of the necessary materials to extract them in the medical department. After cleansing and numbing my leg- she took an instrument that resembled a pair of scissors and tried to grab hold of the fragments. Within a matter of minutes, she said, "*Mr. Mills, you are all done.*" I requested to see the bullet fragment and she obliged. It was a piece of lead that was covered with blood and skin. My eyes were amazed that I had been walking around for 21 years with this apart of my body.

As I sat there being bandaged up—I thought God has allowed me to survive things that a lot of people don't come back from. The little bit of discomfort that I was in didn't compare to the joy that I felt. As I walked to back to my cell, I heard the voice of God and the message was clear: *I can remove all of the negative things in your life that appeared to be permanently apart of you, but I had to get you in an isolated place with no distractions, and I can make sure you come out of this place in your life better than which you entered.* One of the guards asked me why I was skipping down the hallway with a gigantic smile on my face, especially with a bandaged leg, and I said. "*You wouldn't understand.*" After a few days, I was informed that I would be moving to my next job.

The Dock

"And whatever you do, do it heartily, as to the Lord and not to men" **Colossians 3:23 (NKJV)**

I finally met with the work release department and I was granted permission to work on the dock... On the morning of my first official work day—I noticed that Neil was up at 5am praying, reading, and writing in his Bible. I asked him about it and he said that talking to God in the morning set the tone for each day. I told him that some days are hard to communicate with God. He said if you were free, you would be communicating with people via technology, specific email etc. I quickly said; *we don't have access to social media* and he said, *yes, we do* and started laughing. He said, *"Rashad, we have knee mail."* Before I figured it out, he said *knee mail* is kneeling in a prayer-like motion and talking to God through prayer. He would have a scripture of the day that he would write down and commit to memory. I quickly become an imitator and found myself doing it every day. In the worse environment and predicament of my life—I developed a routine that would be forever embedded in my life.

He was a former U.S. soldier and you can see the daily discipline that he showed in all areas of his life. For example, he folded a bed better than anyone I have seen in my life. It was so tight that you could bounce a quarter off of it. It's amazing how my work ethic increased as a result of watching Neil work. It wasn't a coincidence that I was placed in an environment that allowed me to see my own flaws, in addition to having the opportunity to work on them. Every day he worked as if he was getting a raise, and indeed, he wasn't. We were all working for 4 quarters, 10 times, 20 nickels, 100 pennies, or one dollar. However, his work ethic was incredible and I've only seen one person in my life that worked harder, which was my grandfather. The other inmates, correctional officers, and workers who delivered the food noticed it. Since his departure from Jail—I haven't seen him and nor have had the opportunity to say thank you to him for his awesome example.

For an individual like myself who has struggled with discipline, I appreciate the change that I had to develop courtesy of him. The work on the dock wasn't hard but it was humbling, to say the least. We were responsible for unloading the trucks that brought the food in the jail, sorting it out, and then transferring it to the cafeteria. One of my jobs was to wash and empty the trash cans. I would grab the hose and spray the cans and the power of the water would cause the trash debris to fly back and hit me in the face. I would often say to myself that if I was subject to this level of humility that God was preparing me for something much bigger and I had to be ready for it.

During the slow periods—we would engage in pushups contest and use the heavy containers of cooking oil as dumbbells. We would discuss our plans upon release, and of course, one of mine was releasing a book to encourage someone to turn their test into a testimony. All of the snacks that were served in the jail were delivered on the dock and I loved it. I must admit that we munched on potato chips, cookies and we even found a way to get to the commissary snacks like cupcakes and Reese's Peanut Butter Cups. After a few days, I was getting bored with the docks. I became more defiant with some of the orders that were given to us. One supervisor, who was always on a power trip told us to clean the grates after we had completed our work. I was totally against it because I viewed it as pointless because they would be dirty in a matter of hours. Once again—I was in a situation that I couldn't control and—*I hated it!*

Neil pulled me aside one day and asked me if God would be pleased with my work ethic. I was so stunned that I didn't offer a response but I thought about it every day during my stay and upon my release. Since I was a veteran in terms of moving from one job to another, I decided it was time to move on. Before I moved on—I couldn't forget the experience of ending my shift and walking back in the building with the hopes of returning to my tier to take a nap. I didn't think anything would be out of the normal. I knew I had to go through one of the most degrading inhumane processes of all and be stripped searched.

This wasn't new to me because I had been stripped searched on multiple occasions while being detained. But for some reason—this interaction was extremely uncomfortable! It was time for a random urine analysis, which wasn't an issue for me because I didn't use drugs at all. The challenging part was I had just emptied my bladder before entering the work release building again. This particular sergeant wasn't hearing me at all. He made the statement, *"Mills, you have two hours to produce a sample or you're going to lock up because it's considered a refusal."* Refusal?? Not quite—I can't go at the moment. He retorted, *"you better start some drinking water and your two hours start NOW."* Despite my feelings of frustration—I knew that I had to do something quick, so I responded with the question, *"where is the water?"* The sergeant kindly pointed to the sink in the bathroom where inmates are stripped searched at. My mind froze momentarily with the thought of drinking from a discussing sink. Jail isn't exactly the cleanest place on the earth. I have witnessed inmates spit in the sink and not wipe it out. Without another sensible option, I begin to drink so much water that my stomach started to hurt. I was determined not to allow anything to stop me from continuing my job and maintaining my sanity in an absolutely insane environment.

Eventually, I was able to produce the required sample and return to my unit. I don't know if I was more embarrassed than angry. The embarrassment stemmed from putting myself in a position to be controlled by another individual. As I marched back to my cell- I made a vow to myself to use self-control in order not NEVER be controlled again. Since I was already given my release date—which I wasn't happy with—I was looking for alternative options to getting out much sooner.

The Appeal

"If any of you lacks wisdom, you should ask God, who gives generously to all without finding fault, and it will be given to you." **James 1:5 (NIV)**

My bank account was rapidly decreasing and I had a few hundred bucks left to make an important decision with. I had to determine if I was going to use every dime I had left to my name—and hire a lawyer and for bail if it was granted to me. The lawyer would process the *Habeas Corpus*, which is a term meaning that an individual has been wrongly imprisoned. I was confident that a judge would see that a mistake was made and I would be immediately released. The other option would be to invest the money in insurance for a work release job outside of the facility. The amount of insurance was exactly the amount of money that I had left in my account. Due to the efforts of my brother Will getting me a job, I would be afforded the chance to leave the jail every day under my own supervision and return later that evening for work. Both options had pros and cons, but I was leaning towards the *Habeas Corpus*. After conversing with my cell buddies—I was informed that the *Habeas Corpus* couldn't be processed because I was already sentenced.

Just for confirmation purposes, I spoke with a lawyer on the phone and he was willing to move forward but he advised that *"either way"* it's a gamble. I allowed anxiety to get the best of me for several days, even to the point of being angry and pressing my bunk (sleeping) for days. I leaned not on my own understanding, but on that of God—and he advised me to invest in the insurance for the job. It would provide me with an opportunity to acclimate myself again to the work world and handle some of my affairs during my *"free time."* God is so good because I realized that getting out ahead of schedule would have hindered me from learning all of the lessons that were intended for me to learn. I was having a conversation with God and I realized that three times I made efforts to be released, but all of them failed. I was led to the Bible, where specifically *2nd Corinthians 12:8* spoke to my heart in an immeasurable way. 8: Three times I pleaded with the Lord to take it away from me. 9: But he said to me, *"My grace is sufficient for you, for my power is made perfect in weakness."* Therefore, I will boast all the more gladly about my weaknesses, so that Christ's power may rest on me. I felt God would not release me early so I can see that his grace was sufficient and I would rely solely on him.

This gives me a personal strength that I didn't know existed. I was in jail, effectively coping with the stressors of jail and the ability to effectively do it because of the love that God has for me. The appeal (*De Novo*) in Latin means a second time, afresh or a new day. I still entered with the hopes of getting the three years' probation reduced. I didn't want any of this to hinder me and my life going forward. Strangely enough, the appeal was granted but the court date was scheduled for the day after I got out. Within 24hrs of being released, I would have to be back in court to attempt to reduce the three years of probation that I was placed on.

The Church

"The Lord hears the needy and does not despise his captive people." **Psalm 69:33 (NIV)**

Although I connected with God on another level from constant study and prayer—I also believe that church is within the individual and not what occurs just within four walls. I had inquired on several occasions about the church and I was advised to fill out a *one-eighteen*. The one-eighteen form serves as a starting point for anything that you need or want in jail. The chances are high that your concern will no longer be valid by the time they respond to you. For instance, I lost my bath towel and I needed another one. Of course, the correctional officers wouldn't respond in a timely manner because not everyone understands the importance of drying off a shower.

As I approached the correctional officers on a daily basis to check the status—their response would be standard in nature, *"Mills, I don't know yet and when I do—I will let you know."* It is important to know that many of the correctional officers treated the inmates with much respect and sincere concern. Many of the officers saw us as individual human beings—not just a six-digit inmate number. Before the request was granted—I went for two long weeks without a towel using my bed sheet to dry off. So, each night, I would dry off with my bed sheet and then wash and dry it. The other instance that a one-eighteen went unnoticed was my request to be involved in a formal church service. At the time—I didn't understand the significance of the numbers *118* until I was released and one of the sisters in Christ informed me.

Ephesians 1:18 *NIV: "I pray that the eyes of your heart may be enlightened in order that you may know the hope to which he has called you, the riches of his glorious inheritance in the saints."* With every "one-eighteen" request that went unnoticed, my hope would diminish that my needs would get addressed. After learning of this verse, I got reassurance that being detained was leading me to my calling. It was designed to give me hope that I never knew existed. My hope was now planted in the belief that I can survive any situation in life as a result of God backing me. Eventually, the request was granted and I was able to attend a Sunday service. After waking up from a nap, I was called, along with a big portion of my unit to attend church service. I was happy to see so many of the brothers desiring to see the face of God. However, I would later find out that for many it was an excellent opportunity to sell drugs, and further their personal agendas while claiming to be needing God.

After being checked for weapons, I was walking across the gym to seat in the front row. Before I got there—I was stopped and greeted by one of the ministers with the firmest handshake and hug that I had ever received in my life. There was something about the way that he greeted me that led me to believe he was familiar with being an inmate. Prior to the end of service, he would disclose that he was detained for 15yrs and how prison made him into a better person. When I sat down, I could hear the words from the song, *"Just Want You."* by Travis Greene. It was something about the environment and atmosphere that sent chills throughout my body. I found myself rocking back and forth in the chair, which was a clear indication that I was being moved. Maybe it was the lyrics, *"take, everything- I don't want it- I don't need it, God, I just want you."* I looked up and saw the summer evening sun that was shining ever so brightly through the jail bars at the uppermost window of the gymnasium. The sun was God's way of telling me that *I'm shining brightly on your life, despite your current circumstances.*

It was a confluence of emotions that overtook me and I start to cry like a newborn baby. It was so refreshing to let the tears flow like a river. It was an indelible moment in my life that often draws me into a deep sanctuary of the mind. I would attend the services regularly because it enhanced my already growing relationship with God. In jail, somethings occur without sufficient rhyme or reason. For instance, the moment when I was told by a correctional officer that my name was no longer was on the church attendee list. My initial reaction was utter shock, mixed in with anger, but I quickly figured out a better solution. Did I need the assistance of the jail staff to spread the word with my fellow inmates? Absolutely not! Throughout the course of the upcoming week—I would tell my entire unit about Sunday Bible Study on the basketball court.

We would take exercise mats and sit on the basketball court (which was the size of a living room) and discuss our devotionals and success and struggles from the previous week. Some of the inmates who expressed their non-belief suddenly were stopping in out of curiosity. Many of them who had never picked up a basketball used this time to increase their jump shot and free throw percentage. I was laughing to myself and saying thank you, God. His work was being done and brothers were exposed to the word. One of the best examples of walking in purpose and using the opportunity to help others while you are doing it—is Pistol. Pistol was a self-described killer and high-ranking member of one of the most notorious street and prison gangs. He was young (21-25yrs old) and full of venom and street bravado. His presence on the unit caused a disruption because he wanted to run it, specifically as it relates to being on the phone. From a distance, he appeared to be extremely insecure because he wanted his reputation to precede him. He would even go to extreme measures to show his court documents where he killed someone. We never exchanged words with the exception of, *"are you done with the microwave?"* When I would read my Holy Bible on the unit, I could see a level of intrigue from him. I would always pray for the opportunity to introduce him to God. On his lengthy phone calls—I heard him say, *"he is thanking God for another opportunity."*

A few weeks later, I was working out on the basketball court and came out and begin to shoot as well. We gave each other a quick head nod as if to say what's up. Moments later, he started a conversation about court and legal proceedings. I quickly told him that my knowledge was limited in that area. Much to my surprise, we were talking about our individual cases. He was shocked about my detainment, then he asked me why I do read the bible so much and I offered him the following: *It's a road map to life.* I think I shocked him based on his facial expression. For the next hour—I emptied my brain about how good God is, even though we were in jail. He was receptive to all of the information and even thanked me when he left. As soon as he left—I screamed, *"Thank you, God!!"* From this point going forward, we would speak and offer each other encouraging words. I wanted to pray with him prior to his last day, which I started doing to all of my brothers. This was interrupted as he was sent to lock up for an argument with a correctional officer and then he was sent to prison. I hope he knows I'm rooting for him!

On one Sunday morning, the multi-purpose room was at full capacity because all of the curious inmates made their presence felt by coming in. It was beautiful. Could it be that my mistakes served an opportunity to help someone else better themselves? This feeling made my jail time worth it! Toward the conclusion of the Bible study—one of the correctional officers stood on the outside of the room and looked in, paused, and then flashed the biggest smile ever. She opened the door, then apologized for interrupting and then said, *"I have been working in jails and prisons for over 20 years and have never witnessed this type of voluntary involvement. I'm impressed and it's beautiful to see."* A lot of inmates would periodically ask me questions about God and since I'm not an expert, I would answer them to the best of my ability. Prior to my detainment—I wanted to be involved in a jail/prison ministry. God truly has a sense of humor because he provided me with an opportunity.

The Taste of Freedom

"So, if the Son sets you free, you will be free indeed." **John 8:36 (NIV)**

After the community corrections department visited the work site, I was granted the long-awaited permission to go out and work. This job will be different for me because I was given the opportunity to experience a level of freedom, or so I thought. The work release department has specific instructions for inmates who were allowed to go outside of the jail. They provided you with a bus schedule and bus route that allow you to get to work in the shortest time possible. Even if you knew a faster and most convenient bus route—you were not allowed to use it. I completely understand the thought of understanding where an inmate is at all times. However—I felt like a petulant child under the strict supervision of a parent. It was made clear to me that I could leave from the jail at 7:30am (depending on the mood of the correctional officer) and return by 7:00pm. Going into stores wasn't an option either. You were supposed to get on the bus and go to work. No exceptions! I couldn't believe that I was *"free"* and couldn't walk into a store or go to lunch or get a cup of coffee. Walking into a store of my choice was breaking the law.

One of those humbling moments for me was getting on the bus to get to work. I hadn't been on the bus in quite a while and I wasn't sure if I knew how to do it. I quickly found out and adapted. My mother had dropped off some of the work clothes so my attire felt somewhat normal and not the oversized jail jumpers. Not only were the bus routes and hours closely monitored but the amount of your money as well. You were given a weekly allowance of $60 and in addition to that, room and board was taken out of your check! Let me get this straight—I was detained, but yet and still I was paying actual *rent* to the jail? Unbelievable! Prior to my detainment—I knew that the correction industry was a business, where a lot of people would profit—but this was shocking to me. At the moment when I thought I was making significant progress mentally with the situation—I was quickly taken aback on the first day of being an intern at my job. Sometimes I believe God will place you in or near an environment to see if you have learned anything at all.

The bus route to my job required that I passed my former church every day. There were days I stood on the bus stop with pure vengeance shooting from my heart. How could God *do this to me?* Even as I tried to heal? What's the point of this lesson? God was still healing me through his love. After enough rides past the church—it didn't affect me at all, which was a sign of the restoration work that God was doing in my life.

Due to my eagerness to get out of jail, I never questioned the job description that I had at the real estate office where I was assigned. I reminded myself that I served coleslaw, washed dinners, unloaded food trucks, and separated trash—so I could do *anything*. I walked in the door noticing a really big guy with an even larger voice—and on top of that—he seemed to be an even bigger personality. That was my boss! Within the first five minutes—I met several really beautiful women— and after living with way too many men—they were a sight for sore eyes. I kept my wits about me and managed to stay focused on working diligently. After our initial conversation, my boss shared his love for food, sports and helping others because he served years in prison himself. He was more than understanding of the challenges that an inmate faces and he was even more willing to extend his helping hand. This was exactly what I needed and it was refreshing.

I had access to the internet and could use my time to get some of my personal affairs in order like to obtain a lawyer. My boss told me that one of his good friends was a lawyer. I contacted and inquired about his services. He fees were manageable but I was flat broke. (*God will always provide when you need him*) Earlier in the year—I had provided some mental health services to a school and the funds were placed in an account that I completely forgot about allowing me to use that money to obtain good counsel. I was taking any more chances.

He told me I would be responsible for answering the phones, in addition to a few other small tasks. Within the few weeks or so, he treated me to the finest finery in the area and my stomach was highly appreciative. I had waffles (one of my favorites) eggs, bacon, buffalo wings, coffee, sushi, donuts, etc. I immediately programmed myself not to eat any more jail food. For a few fleeting moments—I felt like I was free. The feeling didn't last long when I was faced with the craving for coffee. For anyone that knows me—they know coffee is such a vital part of my morning. On the bus ride, I made up my mind that I was "sneaking" into a coffee shop and I didn't care if the community corrections pulled up one of their check-in rounds and saw me. I got off the bus and darted across the street, looking back as if I just committed a murder. I hurried in, ordered my coffee, and then ran into the building to start my workday. Working was an awesome experience and allowed me to slowly assimilate back into the real world. I hated to leave work each day for a variety of reasons. One, the main reason was the stigma of being an inmate resurfacing constantly.

Each day when I boarded the bus—I had to make sure I had my bus pass in my hand prior to getting on the bus. I was so fearfully that I would drop my id bracelet containing my picture and inmate number and I didn't want anyone to know. Also, I didn't want to drop my walking papers. Community corrections were adamant that each inmate should never be without his walking papers at any point when being off the jail grounds. Walking papers were documents that stated you are property of *the* Baltimore Community Detention Center. It was symbolic of slavery, to say the least. If you didn't have the papers with you and you encountered any police—you were considered an escapee. I often used the bus rides back to the jail to contemplate several pressing things mindfully.

More times than not—I would consider how I allowed myself to make mistakes that jeopardized basic freedoms, that I previously took for granted. The clothing guidelines were so strict that I had 3 dress shirts and two pairs of pants. This meant that I would be wearing the same clothing over and over, and depending on the access to the washing machine on the unit—I might be wearing dirty clothes. Sometimes washing them in the sink inside of your cell wasn't sufficient enough. I devised a plan to get around it by having someone bring me extra clothes that I could keep at the job and I would switch clothes some mornings. If I was released early enough—I would catch a bus that allowed me to be the first one in the building. If this happened, I would race to the office- grab a shirt, head towards the bathroom and then change. On this particular morning—Catherine who worked in the building on another real estate team- saw me going in with one shirt one and coming out with another. She was very nice, quick-witted and sarcastic and that's the reason we become friends. She said, *"Rashad, why do I see you always switching shirts; are you homeless?"* I laughed it off but it was devastating for me because it served as a reminder— I'm not officially free.

This summer was one of the rainiest summers in this history of Baltimore. There was a stormy instance that I vividly remember. I was waiting for the final bus to go back to jail. My clothes made me feel like I was carrying an additional 20 pounds because of the constant pressure of the rain. The raindrops felt like rocks hitting me and I can't see two feet in front of me. Despite the limitations in my physical site that occurred, my internal vision increased greatly. I started to envision this book and the things that I could do upon my release to empower and inspire the next *Rashad Mills*. As a result of this, I had my mother bring me a raincoat and umbrella and backpack to carry it in. I thought it was harmless and smart on my behalf because I was tired of getting soaked at the bus stop. I had to hide the umbrella behind a convenience store before I entered the jail at night and hope it was still available the following morning. Apparently, I didn't know to bring in a book bag in that wasn't authorized by the jail was a violation. The book bag was placed in a locker in the work release department. Later one evening during the nightly rounds—a correctional officer said, I couldn't go to work and there was not any more information. I was worried because I thought an inmate planted something illegal in my locker. Mrs. Bison, the lead community corrections department officer, meet with me the following day for interrogation. The conversation started with her reminding me of my reputation for being a smart mouth to the guards (at times) and with anyone else who tested me along my correctional path. At that point—I know I was still a work in progress and my detainment was helping me.

It felt like I was on trial; Bison was trying to get me to admit to bringing in drugs or weapons. The bookbag was considered contraband and I was placed on hold and not allowed out of the building for three days-time. I begin to pray even harder for sunnier days and it had nothing to do with the weather. Thankfully, I was given clearance to return to work and it was such a blessing. I was even allowed to work on Saturdays. The majority of my time was on the outside and not stuck inside. Upon entering the jail each night—I would see more young men that I used to counsel. Due to my attire, they believed I was providing therapy for other inmates. It was quite the opposite. I had a schedule that consisted of going to my cell, reading the bible in between sets of pushups and sit-ups, showering, having a limited conversation—then heading to bed. It helped the days go by faster. One day after work—I decided to do something that I promised myself that I wouldn't do. I slid to the correctional officer desk and asked them to check my release date. My stomach bubbled slightly and then she gave me the date. I was thrilled that it wasn't too far away—and I knew I could make it.

The Visits

"I needed clothes and you clothed me, I was sick and you looked after me, I was in prison and you came to visit me." **Matthew 25:36 (NIV)**

Having the experience of visiting people in jail before, I always felt a certain level of appreciation from them. Even if the conversation wasn't overly stimulating or important or even if they weren't returning to the community any time soon; it did them wonders to know they were appreciated and that someone took the time to visit. My initial visitor list only included my mom and Will. You had to wait 90 days to make any changes. Each Sunday, Mom and Will would arrive early and offer words of encouragement, updates on the twins and just provide a sense of calm.

For my mother, Pamela Mills, this scene was too familiar. Taking the time out of her schedule, going through scanners and entering jail to see one of her loved ones. I didn't even mention the emotional stress, especially with me, because we didn't see this coming. This had to be a nightmare for her and Deja vu in the worse way. If anyone has the right to be an *anti-jail visits*—it's my mother. She suffered a traumatic experience that still affects her occasionally. When I was old enough to comprehend, she would share not-so-great stories on visits to my father in the late '70s at a federal prison in Marion, Illinois. She had her coat taken by jail authorities because someone planted drugs in it. She had to travel back to Baltimore via van, with a young son (my brother) coatless, cold and scared. Her visiting tour included stops at federal prisons in Oxford, Wisconsin and Lewisburg, Pennsylvania. The coat wasn't the issue because of its material in nature, but it was the mental burden that it caused. As I walked up the steps for a Sunday morning visit with my mom—I experienced a surreal moment. I started to recall all the tension that my mom must be feeling seeing me as my father. I arrived at the thick plexiglass before my mother entered the visiting room and I sat on the hard metal seat and looked at the micro-sized holes that you had to speak through to be heard. My heart started to beat so fast. I knew I had messed up in a major way.

When my mom walked in and prepared to sit down—the beautiful, slender, face of my mother quickly turned into a canvas for future tears. I said to myself, she won't be able to make it twenty minutes without crying. After the standard conversation and giving the motherly advice of trusting God, reading my bible, and not arguing with the guards and other staff, it happened! She gave me an awkward look as if she was a ghost, and started to say something that I couldn't understand. Her lips were trembling and in between the tears, I was able to decipher the words: You look like your father sitting there. It was like a bomb had just gone off. The flow of tears was now a rainstorm. She expressed how mistakes ruined my father and she didn't want that for me and how my girls didn't deserve to grow without a father present and endure the pain that my brother and I had to. At this point—we were crying in unison. I tried to comfort her but it was too heartbreaking for her and she continued to sob uncontrollably. As the guard gave the signal letting her know the visiting time had concluded—we both stood up and motioned a kiss to each other. As I walked back down the steps and into my cell, the following thoughts entered my mind—my mother *really* has my back.

For the majority of my life—my mother and I have had a lukewarm relationship at best. I have desperately sought the attention of a woman to replace that of my mother. As a single parent mother raising two kids, she did an incredible job with my brother and I. Yet due to the overwhelming duties she was faced with—she wasn't present at the PTA meetings and baseball games and there was a small piece of resentment directed at her. I feel like I sought, and craved that attention in a mate, even to the point in relationships that I would be more engaged in my mate's well-being more than my mothers. My mother would openly admit to me that she was jealous of the relationship with my ex-friend because of the attention and generosity I would give.

When she revealed this to me—my initial shock was quickly overcome with the understanding that she was looking for the same thing I was: love from a parent. I happened to be the closest man to her at the present time that she could receive attention from. Mending our relationship continues to be an important goal for me, especially considering my lack of communication that my brother and mother have. My brother is a kind-hearted spirit that has felt like the black sheep of the family. He has made financial investments to family members that have caused him great hardship. In addition to this, he has never been able to forgive my father for not being present in our lives. In a moment of anger—he even mentioned that he wanted to change his name to distance himself from my father. I really believe, he too, longed for my father as a child but he hasn't reached the level of forgiveness that I have.

My maternal grandfather was largely not present. My grandmother was left raising three girls on her own. That coupled with the sexual abuse she suffered as a child, probably contributed to her attempting to cope by drinking and becoming an alcoholic. My grandmother had the biggest heart and was one of the nicest people that you would ever want to meet. At one point she lived with us and every morning she would wake up and cook breakfast for all of my friends. It was a buffet style spread every morning and I loved it. She had an infectious spirit about it. I begin to see trends with substance abuse as a coping mechanism for trauma throughout my family. I honestly believe that she didn't have the tools to give attention to my brother and me—although she provided us with all of the necessities. It was trying to give something that she didn't have. Her love never manifested itself to give attention, but I understand it better now.

My mother has never recovered from the abandonment from her father and every relationship since his absence has suffered as a result of it. My mom and dad married and divorced twice and although they truly love each other—the lack of forgiveness and hurt are hurdles that are hard to get over. My father's incarceration left a young mother with the strenuous task of raising two kids by herself. My mom has held onto those emotions for years. I used to think she should get over it—but I have to validate her feelings and experiences—which are all very real. Even to this present day—often watch my mother battle symptoms of depression. Sometimes, I become overwhelmed with sadness at the thought that her personal goals in her life have never been fulfilled because she had so much responsibility on her plate. Sometimes, I see her as a frightened little girl scared to go after the life and level of success that's rightfully hers. I think her ambition is always impeded by the fear of failure and getting outside her comfort zone. Prior to my detainment, I would find myself playfully hugging her and I could instantly feel and sense of peace and calm take over.

For years, I have been on the end *of "you get on my nerves like your father"* comments—due to the almost twin-like resemblance we share. I know they are intended to be innocuous, but I also know the pain that pushes them to be said. Unless the broken family's issues are recognized, addressed, and healed—the continuation of them will affect more generations.

Interestingly enough, during the darkest moments of my life—my mother was the most supportive women in my corner. My mother witnessed me graduate from one of the most prestigious universities in the world (*Johns Hopkins* in 2015) with a master's degree; this same woman was there to support me as an inmate.

Many of the bunk buddies would question how I got so many visits and especially after normal hours. Some would joke and say—I must be an undercover cop. Luckily for me, the majority of my visits would come from my colleagues in the mental health field. I personally think they would be more shocked than me. Due to the professions of psychiatrists, mental health therapists and social workers, I was allowed professional visits. They showed up every week with hearts filled with love and support. I could see disappointment, concern, and uncertainty on their faces as well. A few of them figured that I must have violated the initial protective order to be sentenced to jail. They would later realize that I didn't and it was a part of a bigger mission and learning lesson. Interestingly enough, one of the biggest supporters was William Batts. William had previously reached out to me to be a guest on his show (*On the Couch Radio*) to discuss mental health issues. We had a great time on the show and from that point—we had connected and he surprised me visiting once a week and offering all the love that a brother could. Prior to the detainment—he served as my personal therapist for sometimes two hours at a time.

He always encouraged me to see my ex-friend's actions from the potential illness and not the person. I could only see my own level of hurt and nothing else. During this period—I couldn't operate as Rashad the therapist because it was too personal for me. His ears should still be tired from all of the listening. He was and remains a Godsend. Every week I got multiple letters from my extended work family. The letters ranged from Dr. M reminding me to use my coping skills and deep breathing exercises. Nana T sent me sermons she heard-even with a move out of state, she still set aside time for me. Dr. S provided letters and a desire to help me in any way possible. Artie L forced me to examine my personal flaws during my downtime. I was blessed by the abundant outpouring of love. My aunt C. Mills sent little index-sized cards with thought-provoking messages.

Rashad,

Glad to hear that you can see light at the end of the tunnel. Please do not be fooled into believing this light (27th) is the end of this journey. In reality, this journey has just begun and the key is not to return.

Whatever you do, avoid at all cost police, courts, or anything that places your life in jeopardy. Anything or anybody.

-DAD

Rashad,

It was great seeing you and how you are using this experience to nurture your spiritual growth. I could feel how grounded and centered you are.

-Dr. M

Hey Bro Rashad,

Although you may not be in the place that you want to be, you can still be used for greater. In fact, I believe you will have more of a testimony than ever before and then even more people will be touched and delivered through whatever they may be going through because of your story and boldness. I'm so sorry you're in this situation but know it's only temporary and it doesn't dictate your future.

Shantee M

Rashad,

Miss you! I know you have been way further than this before and you'll come out on top of the whole situation. That being said my wish is for you to keep your mind together while you are there. I wish for you to find some people there you can pray with and preach to. Maybe you have a mission to touch someone in there-or maybe there is a soul there that will touch you in some way.

-Christine B

Moving on doesn't mean forgetting,
It means you choose happiness over hurt.
Aunt Catherine

Rashad,

To see you in tears last week really touched me. I know this hard on you, but just remember, our thoughts are not God's thoughts. I don't know the reason for all of this, but you have to trust God. God has something good for your life, but sometimes, he takes us through the process. And the process sometimes can be hard and stressful.

-Mom

Rashad,

-We are saved BY grace Through faith

-God uses uncomfortable situations so we can rely on him.

-Sometimes the pain is the antidote to our real problem. This keeps us from getting to a place that will destroy us

-His grace will shape you

-Keep pushing good brother. God will provide you with the strength

-Nana T

Dear Rashad,

I hope this time away helps you to heal mentally(emotionally) and physically. I am praying that God also heals you spiritually. I am sure that this will be another powerful testimony that you can and will share with your audience(s). I know that you have lost (or will) lose a number of things during this process, but I am sure you will gain more- you just have to stay on course and trust the process. Plus, you are so influential and strong, I don't see you staying down for long. I hope you get a chance to use this time, to release all emotions stemming back from your childhood-where the real hurt happened.

-Artie L

My Devotional Writings

(As written)

7/12/18 9:45am

Prior to the start of this morning, bible study, I'm elated to have yet another opportunity to share in the Word of God.

This gives me comfort because prior to coming out of my cell—I struggled to find any meaning in my detainment.

What's your Passion?

7/18/18

Today's devotional is focused on your passion. Strangely enough, today is my 3rd year of sobriety. Alcohol used to be my passion. But today God is my passion. Thank God for sobriety.

Psalm 20:7 *Some trust in chariots and some in horses but we trust in the name of the Lord our God.*

8/6/18

Today's devotional is falling. Clearly, I've fallen to a degree which has landed me in jail. However, the Word provides hope.

Proverbs 24:16 *For a righteous man may fall seven times and rise again- but the wicked shall fall by calamity.*

8/13/18

Today's devotional is dedicated to wisdom in witnessing. Interestingly enough—bible study conducted on the tier on 8/12/18 was about witnessing to other inmates. I thank God for 15 more people for next Sunday's bible study! People see us and become interested.

Matthew 5:16 *Let your light so shine before men, that they may see your good words, and glorify your father in heaven.*

9/28/18

Today's devotional is about asking God first. This is my first full day as a free man after 101 days of being in the Baltimore County Detention Center. I'm asking God first to give me direction on all things of my life at this point.

Psalm 37:4 *Delight yourself also in the Lord. And he shall give you the desires of your heart.*

The Fear

"So do not fear, for I am with you; do not be dismayed, for I am your God. I will strengthen you and help you. I will uphold you with my righteous right hand." **Isaiah 41:10 (NIV)**

As the seconds, minutes, hours, weeks, and months came closer to my release date—I figured I was ready. More importantly, I trusted God's timing for me and I believed I would walk out when it was appropriate. September 27, 2018, couldn't arrive fast enough. In the last weeks and days before my release- I felt my anxiety becoming more of an issue than before. Years ago, I remember reading an article from a popular men's magazine about an aging bank robber. He spent significant time in prison (40 years) altogether, and upon his release, he robbed another bank. The article stated that after robbing the bank, he sat in his car for three minutes and waited to be arrested. Two and half days later- he was arrested and told the arresting officers, "Just take me home. I want to go home now." The home he was referring to was jail. He was adamant to remind the cops he used a loaded gun, which could give him twenty more years. I could never understand this way of thinking, which I used to think was insane.

I had a flashback of the phone calls from jail that I would get from my father and his level of comfort was much higher being detained, as opposed to being free. But now it made a lot of sense. The starting over can be just as mentally taxing as the initial detainment. I could imagine what this is like for women and men who were detained for much longer periods than me. Jail provides a level of comfort as it relates to food and housing. The food is awful and the housing most definitely is no mansion—but it's guaranteed as long you're there. You cannot be evicted. I was barely hanging on to my housing on the outside world and I didn't have a job to sustain all of my expenses.

In what would seem a perfect job fit for me; the county had an opening for a therapist position. I was informed that some of the administration in the juvenile justice department shot down the idea of bringing me back as a therapist. My surprise and disappointment were more for the men I could serve; as my offenses were not a normally incarcerating circumstance. I honestly believe that my story resonates with the young men even more because I experienced it on a personal level within that very criminal justice system.

In addition to this, I knew in jail I didn't have to worry about bills and trying to be successful. My initial concerns of mentally adjusting to freedom, being a mentally present father, and the stigma of being a newly released inmate weighed heavily on my mind. Upon my release—I would have a new response to the question of, "*have you ever been detained?*" I was preparing to be judged by certain circles of people from now on.

Despite all of the challenges of being free—I was looking forward to the basic freedoms of cooking food for myself and showering in a bathroom minus six other guys. I got excited about sleeping in a bed that is mine and not hearing the constant commotion of other inmates, guards and metal doors slamming all hours of the night. I was thankful to God that he had given me a fresh start in my life again. With all of the pleasurable things in life that I was looking forward to—there was a small part of me that was afraid. The fear was leaving the strange comfort that I got accumulated to. For someone who wasn't previously familiar with jail—I found myself in a state of mind that was actually afraid to go out and start again. As a man of great faith—I had to break that line of thinking that momentarily took over. One of my favorite scriptures is **Hebrews 11:1** (*NIV*) *Now faith is confidence in what we hope for and assurance about what we do not see.* The level of self-reflection grew deeper as the realization that "*the freedom*" our ancestors used to reflect upon at the old Watch Night Service celebrating New Year's Eve—was at hand for me.

The Decision

"Be Kind to another, tenderhearted, forgiving one another, forgiving each other, just as Christ God forgave you." **Ephesians 4:32 (NIV)**

Within a week of being released—I returned to jail after another day of work release and my energy wasn't what I would have expected, considering my immediate future. I remember dragging myself to my bunk and attempting to shut off the jail sounds that I was normally accustomed to, but more importantly, my own inner thoughts. The overly happy moments of pending freedom were being overshadowed by incredible regret, anger, and lack of forgiveness that were directed towards me. I had never verbalized those in great detail to anyone other than God. It was almost as if I was running away from my wrongdoing because it was easier to justify being detained at the hands of someone else.

Throughout my detainment—I was always aware of the reason that I got there—however I don't think I ever accepted full responsibility. The old saying still holds true that it takes two to dance. It became easier to sidestep the idea that I was flawed and I needed work and jail was my place for healing. There was one particular inmate by the name of Carlin, who gave me the most brutally honest reality check about me and my current situation. We were on the basketball court shooting hoops and we struck up a conversation. Carlin was in his early fifties and was one of the more pleasant and funnier inmates in the unit. With the level of peace that he seemed to have inside and out—I was sure he was a man of God. And indeed, he was. Just like the entire jailhouse building—he had lapses in judgment and made mistakes. Carlin advised me that he smiles so much because he was able to forgive and that God forgives. I stopped shooting the basketball at this point because I had a feeling, he was about to get pretty serious. He said, *"Mills, you know I was facing life plus 50 years."* After I heard this—I wasn't sure I was still breathing. I replied, *"how much time?"* and he repeated it again. I was almost afraid to ask what he did, but he had me completely intrigued.

He said in his slick New York Accent—*"she betrayed me."* My inner thought told me that I knew the feeling. He continued by saying that his girlfriend and one of his former employees conspired to steal a huge sum of money ($32,000) from the safe in his house. Carlin stated he walked in his house after returning home from work and saw them with the safe open. He told me how he immediately grabbed a hold of his registered handgun and shot the guy (didn't kill him) and slammed his wife, breaking furniture in the house. HECK NO! was my response due to the shock of it all. He said it was me. The rest of the story played act like a scene in an action movie. Carlin stated he eluded the police for a period of hours by running in the woods, lakes, even being chased by dogs and followed by the helicopter. After his arrest and subsequent indictment—he thought his life was over. Apparently, God had a better and unexpected plan for his life because he told me he was going to be released after a year. The state didn't have enough evidence. At this point — I was looking at him in amazement. I quickly commented, how could she, and in a mid-sentence—he cut me off. *"Rashad, it's not her and it was me."* He continued by preaching on the importance of self-control. He then enlightened me on how it's one of the fruits of the spirits. **Galatians 5:22-23** (*NIV*) *But the fruit of the spirit is love, joy, peace, patience, kindness, goodness, faithfulness, gentleness, and self-control.*

I'm never at a loss for words but at this point—I was stone silent. I have never discussed my charges with him before. When he asked about my reason for being detained—I told him, and he smiled and said self-control. *"Rashad, you didn't have to call her."* And I embarrassingly nodded my head in the argument. *"No matter what she did or didn't do can't justify your behavior."* I was fuming because the reality had set in that he was right. I fired back with *"she betrayed me, manipulated me, denied me, and controlled me, and all I ever did was love her."* He laughed again. He said I know you read the bible so you are quite familiar with Jesus and Judas. Judas betrayed Jesus for 30 coins. He even reminded me that Jesus washed the feet of Peter, who would go onto to deny him. He was adamant that we all want to be Christlike until we have to demonstrate his characteristics. I was stunned and had no rebuttal because he was speaking the truth and the truth stands by itself. His words were like a boxer's powerful body blows to my entire mindset.

At one point I started to believe something was wrong with Carlin because now the laugh grew louder and louder. *"Control You? She didn't have a gun to your head, did she?* In a low and embarrassing voice—I said *"NO."* *"What was wrong with you? You are a therapist, aren't you?"* I answered yes in the same embarrassing, ashamed tone, *"Yes."*

I'm not sure if I was even listening to him anymore at this point because I was in my own head. I started thinking with the awful feeling of admitting to myself that I was codependent on someone's else love. The attention that she was giving me (whether it was real or fake) fueled my desire to be needed and wanted. It validated me as a person and as a man. I needed her just as much as she needed me. We were dependent upon each other. Two broken people trying to be together and be whole. I wanted to help her become the greatest version of herself because of my love for her, but I think I wanted to feel like I was able to save someone because I was inept in previous relationships. I feel like if I helped her—she would recognize my value and become more attached to me. It was time to admit that my love was not completely unconditional like I thought. We both had ulterior motives. We were both using each other to better ourselves and maybe didn't realize it. All of the behaviors from her and I were trying to meet and fulfill a specific need. Maybe the methods were different but they were equally as wrong.

I really begin to understand myself and my former friend from a much greater lens. I strongly believe that she has been through some difficult events—and in her trying to cope with them as best she could—I came along and lost momentary control as Carlin said. To be completely honest—she is one of the most resilient people I know. Maybe sharing her difficulties with a therapist would cause wounds, memories, and feelings to be opened or reopened and she is not at that place in her life. I quickly reminded myself how long took me to make any significant strides towards my own self-improvement. I was truly not in a position to judge.

Throughout the relationship—I found myself not even thinking for myself. The need to be in a relationship gave away my thinking. I remember cutting off my facial hair because she didn't like. Due to my need for acceptance and approval—I did it. It is easier now to understand how an individual can lose their self-identity trying to go along with someone else's demands set upon them. Sometimes, I believe both of us were in survival mode and operated at the highest level of functioning at that moment. I could see Carlin's lips moving but it was as if I was caught in a trance. My brain replayed in great detail every instance in which the thought of starting off over and being alone probably held both of us in a relationship that we both should have walked away from. Healing can come from the most unexpected people and places. A part of mine took place brilliantly on a basketball court in the county jail.

Luckily for me, another unit called for Carlin and he left. Opening the door, Carlin paused for one last piece of advice, he used his foot to hold it open saying, *"Forgive yourself, and more importantly, forgive her." "Didn't God forgive you?"* Then the sound of the heavy door slamming snapped me back into reality.

I picked up the basketball and started shooting for hours until the correctional officers told me the recreation area was closed. During that time my brain was filled with the reality of my flawed behavior in relationships, particularly the mother of my kids, Christina. In 2008, I met Cynthia and she was filled with all the love that one man could ever want. She was thoughtful, caring and beautiful, inside and out! Christina had all of the elements that make up a great wife, but I was young, immature and certainly didn't understand the value of a good woman. I was insecure in every aspect of my life and my coping skill was alcohol. My insecurity led me to be unsupportive and led her improperly in my role in the relationship. Due to every part of my life being out of control—I attempted to control her, even to the point of being abusive towards her on more than occasion. Blame can't be placed on the alcohol or any other factor. It was simply a broken man attempting to navigate a plethora of emotions and the demons inside of him.

At the time—I didn't know how to express what I felt. I used to be critical of her professional success because I hadn't amassed any noteworthy level of success and I know she would eventually find someone better than myself to care for her better than I could. I didn't have the slightest clue about manhood and what it meant. At that juncture in my life—I was only a man by gender alone. Despite all of this—Cynthia attempted to help me financially, mentally and with fighting my addiction. None of it worked because I hated myself so much.

After our separation and co-parenting challenges (which I caused), she continued to remain a good person despite the demons that I battled. I never thought Cynthia would forgive for me all of the problems that I caused her. One day in a phone conversation—she told me; "*I forgave you because I knew there was something that was driving your behavior. I always knew you were hurting but I didn't know why.*" Even in this present day—my level of discomfort increases tremendously while

I'm in her wonderful presence and she probably doesn't even know it. There is a part me that says, *"Rashad, you were that guy at one point that caused pain, worry, headaches, and sleepless nights to another undeserving person."* When these moments surface—I have to remind myself **1 John 1:9** (*NIV*) *If we confess our sins, he is faithful and just and will forgive us our sins and purify us from all unrighteousness.*

Knowing that my heavenly father forgives me is a source of comfort but what if my kids ever learn and decide not to forgive me? I don't know the outcome of this yet—but I trust God will give me the strength to deal with it in the future.

When I started with the writing of this book—I didn't have the intention or thought—I would be this vulnerable. I worried about being viewed differently, criticized, given dirty looks by some, losing engagements and future opportunities. The fear existed of the way my kids would be viewed as a result of my actions. However; I was getting a constant urge and push to write it and let God sort out the rest.

In my daily practice as a therapist—I'm subjected to hearing countless stories of broken people distributing pain to other people (doesn't always include physical) in an effort to find relief within themselves. Each time—my heart goes out to the abused and the abuser. I know both are hurting for a variety of reasons. I trust God that this book will land in the hands of people that will benefit from it.

The New and Improved

"Therefore, if anyone is in Christ, he is a new creation: the old has gone, the new has come." **2 Corinthians 5:17 (NIV)**

September 27, 2018, will always be an interesting day for me. It was my last day being *inmate 458627*. I was about to experience true freedom and attempt to continue my life. During the previous night—I tossed and turned mightily and I was unable to sleep. I remember getting up and shoving all of my belongings in a net bag and sitting it by the sally port, which is a set of doors that lead to the hallway. My mother had been given the time of 10am to get me, but after all, this was jail and everything is subject to change. I started to play mind games with myself and started counting by one and figuring by the time I got to a certain number—my name would be called. That didn't work. Then, I resorted to doing pushups and that didn't work. I started praying and that didn't work. Eventually, I would climb on the bunk for one last time and reflected on all of the things that have taken place in the last 101 days. *I made it!!! Thank you, God, for keeping me!*

Being released was processed that included returning to the processing area where it started. I sat in one of the same cells that I occupied three months prior and tears almost started to flow. I was going to be able to sit down with my kids and eat. The thought of showering and sleeping was refreshing. Before the dream became a reality—we (other inmates) went through a lengthy process of getting paperwork for our release and returning jail property. I was certainly ready to run out of the building at this point. After sitting in the cell for an hour, we heard a voice. The voice was familiar. It was the voice of the same sergeant who put me through hell to produce a urine sample or I would lose my job. I had to endure him one more time and I figured I would never see him again. He said, *"Alright, Listen Up! This is how this process works"* and he started to give instructions. It was one last reminder that when you are in jail, you have rules to follow. After grabbing my bag (mainly books and bibles) we headed in a single file line to the elevator. It was almost time!

Prior to getting on the elevator—the shackling yellow bracelet, which served as my ID was cut off. Freedom was only minutes away. Seven of us were placed in the elevator and when it would stop— *Rashad Mills* would be free for the first time in 101 days. Just before the sergeant hit the button—he said the following heartless, cold-blooded words, which I will never forget, *"Thank You for your stay at the Baltimore County Hotel. We look forward to your next stay."* *What!?* My happy thoughts of freedom were momentarily interrupted by his devilish comments. What felt like an eternity was only a few seconds in the elevator. Once the door opened, I thought to myself that God allowed me to take the worst experience of my life and come out stronger! Physically, mentally, and emotionally—I am better than I could have imagined. *Won't he do it!*

I walked to the line to get my last check. As I turned around—I saw my mother and tears begin to flow. She was elated and so was I. After another twenty minutes or so—I was free. I drove home and it was an awesome feeling. During the drive home—a police officer got behind me and my heart froze, even though I hadn't done anything wrong. He eventually switched lanes and went on about his business. I was hoping that I wouldn't have to deal with moments like this the rest of my life. My therapist would later diagnose me with Post-Traumatic Stress Disorder (PTSD). After getting home and unwinding and reflecting—I took the longest shower ever. I was able to cook my own food, which I enjoyed thoroughly. I made heartfelt phone calls thanking those who helped me through this ordeal. I thought I would take some time to sit and rest and take a nap. Before I realized it—I was trying to make up time from the previous 101 days. I was trying to schedule speaking engagements, inquire about new employment opportunities and dealing with an anxious mind again. One of the many benefits of the detainment was the ability to be mindful and not worry about the future. Despite the promises that I made to myself—I was right back at it.

I looked at the clock in my kitchen and it was time to be a father again and pick up my kids from my school. I even began to question one of the things that I know I'm good at—which is fatherhood. Could I still be a productive father after what I have been through? Was I mentally ready for the challenge at hand? Would they still love me? One of the biggest fears that I had was the fearing of failing them. I knew if I failed; they would fail as well. I was about to find out. It was a frightening thought! My kids were prepared for me to get them and attend back to school night. I was emotionally overwhelmed for a variety of reasons.

I felt like I was out of touch with them and was starting over. I had missed the first day of school for the first time ever and wasn't familiar with their teachers. My overthinking allowed me to believe that their teachers would think I was an uninvolved and absent father. When I pulled in the parking lot—I got out of my car and ran to the door. It was a nasty day outside with a blustery wind and rain. I had on a windbreaker style jacket with a hood on it. The hood didn't stop the immediate recognition from the girls. Maybe it was my silhouette or walk that caught their attention. As the door opened—I could see the oldest of the twins sprinting to me screaming, "*Daddy!*" When I hugged her—I felt a thump from my blindside like a quarterback being sacked by a defensive lineman. It was her sister! We had a glorious group hug in the middle of aftercare. The car ride home was just like old times with the girls arguing with each other saying "*It's my turn to talk.*" For a brief moment in time—my mind finally stopped worrying and I was able to focus on the two most important people in the world.

Unfortunately—I was unable to remain in this place of peace for long because I was scheduled to be back in court again the next day. My ultimate goal was to reduce the amount of probation that I was subject to. From my experience—I have witnessed many people on probation make the slightest of mistakes and get a one-way ticket back to jail. At all costs—I was desperately trying to avoid it. I was newly released from jail and I dreaded the thought of being in a courtroom again. Additionally, I was going to have seen my ex-friend again. I was not looking forward to that all because I was uncertain of the temperature of her feelings. After going through the metal detector—I heard the jingle of a police officer handcuffs, as he walked behind me. My heart jumped and I gasped in fear. Although there wasn't a real threat present, the possibility of detained again was all too real. When I stepped out of the elevator—I caught the attention of the slim, slickly dressed black guy with a briefcase in his hand. I had never met my lawyer in person but I figured it was him, and indeed, I was right. He pulled me aside and we went over the game plan again, which was to reduce the probation. He was comforting, cool, and very professional. I went into the courtroom to get a seat up front and relax. One of the bailiffs told me that my case was moved to the adjacent courtroom. As soon as I opened the door—I was greeted by my former friend looking at me whispering to a friend, *"he's here."* Not again, I thought to myself. At this point—I walked outside have a talked with my lawyer. I noticed he was talking to the state's attorney and they were both in argument to reduce the probation. My lawyer walked back in the courtroom and due to the years of experience in a variety of situations, my attorney was able to pick up on the energy from my former friend.

He returned asked me questions like, *"Why do you think she is still angry? Do you think she would talk to me?* I answered I don't know to both. He entered the courtroom and asked if she would speak with him in a private area. He *wanted* to inform her the appeal wasn't an attempt to bother her in any way. His facial expression as he exited the courtroom was telling. She informed him that she didn't want to talk to anyone connected with me. I understood it because I couldn't minimize how she felt or what she has been through. She told him that she would make it her business to be at any postponements. I eventually entered the courtroom and sat next to my attorney and waited for my appeal to be heard. I happened to glance in her direction and I felt extremely sad.

I was seeing her for the first time in three months and the lens I was looking at her from was completely different. I believe I was able to see under the beautiful exterior to see an individual who was hurt. I saw an individual who was fearful of the judgment she would be faced with if anyone ever knew that she had a potential mental health illness. My heart yearned because I know the pride that she carries every day and I have no idea if she will ever to be able to address the potential illness without thinking less of herself as a person. I hurt because I'm not even sure if she is aware of some of the behaviors. Just as my feelings took over—I was reminded of one the things she would say to me in her southern twang; *Look at God!* I have to look at God and believe if he allowed me to heal and found revelation; he will surely do the same for her.

After several trips to the judge's bench from both sides—the judge was shocked that nothing could get resolved, especially since I just served time. His final ruling was the probation will remain but after three years—I could get it expunged. As far as the courts and judges were concerned, this felt like closure.

As I quickly walked out of courthouse—I thought of the following: in the darkest days of my life, I was able to develop and experience a true relationship with God, as he protected, guided, and healed me. I went in as a complete mess and left out with a message of how good God really is. And as for *inmate 458627*; it is finished!

Afterthoughts and Reflections

I can never condone my behaviors that led to my detainment. My faulty thinking resulted in a lot of people getting hurt, but I hope this book lands in the hands of someone who will find healing from journey. The vulnerability of writing this book has been one of the toughest things I have mentally endured in my life. The level of self-reflection took me to a place that I have never been to before.

I have the greatest love for those who are suffering from mental illnesses of all kinds. As a therapist and someone who has suffered—I know that healing is possible. You are not alone in this journey. I honestly believe that we are as sick as the secrets that we hide. Healing comes from admitting that issues exist.

I stand firm in the belief that people aren't evil or nasty by nature, but I think we encounter challenges that shape our behaviors, thoughts, and actions. Let's try not to judge knowing that one day soon—we will all be judged by the Master.

For all of my brother and sisters who are detained by bars or suffering with mental challenges—you will be free someday and I LOVE YOU!!!!

Acknowledgements

Thank You God for placing the following people my in life to make this possible.

Mom: You are stronger than I ever imagined!! I appreciate you - even when you don't realize it.

Dad: I appreciate you! Going through this situation has enhanced my love for you. Let's rebound from our mistakes and show the world what a redeemed man looks like.

Love Bugs: Dad made mistakes. Please Forgive. I love y'all!!!

Cynthia: Thank You for being an amazing person despite who have I been. Thank You for demonstrating true forgiveness. Thank you for giving me the Love Bugs

Aunt C: Thank You for being you. Kind and Caring

My Brother: Thanks for housing! I hope one day - we can talk as brothers and not as enemies

William Rodgers: I owe you and can never repay you. You are truly a brother!!! You went above and beyond. You have been instrumental in my life!!

Chuck: My main man. I appreciate you!!!

William Batts: I appreciate you brother!!! The Love is Real!

Jason: From playing touch football as kids to taking me to work when my car died- you have been one of my biggest supporters. I appreciate you champ!!!

LB: My guy from way back!

Aunt T: thank you! You bought the first book!

Jacqueline A: thank you for the daily encouragements with the mother while I was gone

Mike Foy: I remember the conversation in the parking lot giving me support and love. You are a true brother!!!

Sean Wilson: You took a chance on me and I thank you!!! Love you brother

Tarsha: I love you buddy!!!

Sister Beverly: Thank you for your encouraging words of support, and being so good to my babies!!! You are a true sister in Christ!

Rev. Carroll: Thank you!!! It's a part of the plan!

Andrea J: Sis, I love you. You are real, funny, and supportive!

Mel B Cook: Thanks for being real, raw and speaking life into me when I was depressed. I won't forget when you told me- I was more than enough. We have legacies to build.

Sugar Ray Destin, Jr.: Good brother, thanks for being patient while I learned the process of being an author and the positive words.

Shantee and Mark: Love Y'all!!!!

Dr. M: Your peace and guidance helped me tremendously. (That Dog Will Hunt) inside Joke

Dr. S: Millzy (INSIDE JOKE) appreciates you. You are loving and supportive and an amazing woman.

Nana T: The sister that I never wanted (insert smiles and laughter). You are awesome!!! I Love you. You held me down

Artie L: I will never forget the letter you wrote. It helped me tremendously discover how I am. It was like a therapy session

Christine B: I appreciate you!! Let's get two cold kombuchas and talk about life.

Micheline: What's up Mickey? Huggie? When you and the Mayor renew the vows: I got you!

Awesome God Radio (Antoine Jefferson): For not turning me away and still allowing me a platform to praise God. Love you brother!

Awesome God Radio: Sis, Tiffany Barnes: From the PIT TO THE PALACE!!!

Hope Health: Jarv, Jonesy, and Y F. Thank you for the opportunities to continue to serve as therapist!!!

To my former friend: When I met you—I could not have predicted this ending in a million years. This was not my intention to have things happen this way, but I found understanding in the following **Romans 8:28**: *And we know that in **ALL** things God works for the good of those who love him, who have been called according to his purpose.* I thank God for revealing the purpose of this to both of us. I pray you receive this in the right way. I thank you for allowing me to discover the broken and damaged parts that lay within me as a result of our relationship.

More importantly—I thank God for your healing and the beautiful life you will have thereafter!

Resources

Mental Health Resources

www.nimh.nih.gov 1-800-662-HELP (4357)

www.mentalhealth.gov

www.nami.org

www.mentalhealthamerica.net 1-800-273-TALK (8255)

https://suicidepreventionlifeline.org/ 1-800-273-8255

www.Blackmentalhealth.com

Resources for Returning Citizens

F.A.C.E. (Freedom Advocates Celebrating Ex-Offenders)

www.facebaltimore.org

https://www.minorityhealth.hhs.gov/omh/content.aspx?ID=10326

www.cominghomedirectory.org/about-us/

To order additional titles from Rashad:

ORDER FORM

Email form to: rashadspeaks@rashadmills.com

(Please print clearly to ensure prompt delivery)

Ship to:
Mr./Ms./Mrs. _____
Street Address _____
Apartment Number/Suite _____
City _____ State _____ Zip_____
Telephone (_____) _____ - _____

PAYMENT METHOD

I've enclosed a Check/Money Order _____

Credit Card:

**Quantity and Book Title: Cost:
_____ Inmate 458627 $20.00

*Taxes-add 8.25% tax to all orders   *add 4.95/book for shipping

Total Cost: _____

**Special discounts are available on quantity purchases by corporations, associations, educators, and others. For details, contact the publisher at the above listed address.

U.S. trade bookstores and wholesalers: Please contact Rashad Mills

Email rashadspeaks@rashadmills.com

About the Author

Rashad "BOWTIE" MILLS is a child of the Highest God, father of lovable twin girls, licensed mental health therapist, speaker, and community advocate. Rashad holds a Bachelor's of Science Degree in Broadcast Journalism from *Morgan State University* and a Master's of Science Degree in Clinical Community Counseling from *Johns Hopkins University*. Rashad is the host of his own show every Tuesday at 7pm on Awesome God Radio. Also, Rashad is known for his weekly motivational messages on social media known as "Happy Hour." Rashad enjoys reading and long distance running in his spare time.

To book Rashad for your next event:

rashadspeaks@rashadmills.com
rashadmills.com

RASHAD MILLS